A COURSE IN MIRACLES
has been for me one of the most
important contributions to my personal
happiness, clarity, and success.
I agree with those people who
say that it is the most important book
written in the last 2,000 years. I have
developed this workbook of daily
exercises to make The Course easier
to apply to your life.

Sondra Ray

Drinking
the Divine

A Workbook

CELESTIAL ARTS
Berkeley, California

Copyright ©1984 by Sondra Ray

Celestial Arts
P.O. Box 7327
Berkeley, CA 94707

First Printing, October 1984

Made in the United States of America

Library of Congress Catalog Number: 84-045361

ISBN: 0-89087-460-3

3   4   5   6   -   93   92   91

Dedication

I dedicate this book to you Babaji,
Shri Shri 1008 Shri Bhagwan
Hherakan Wale Baba, thou holy
divine master of eternity,
embodiment of joy, I surrender in
complete gratitude.

and

to You, Jesus, my elder brother
who conquered death, with great
respect and appreciation in my
heart forever.

At the feet of both of you, I pray
that everything I write be
something beautiful for God and at
your service.

Contents

Foreword

The purpose of this book is to make it easier for you to study the *Course in Miracles* and, of course, to bring more happiness into your life. I am always trying to inspire people to read the *Course*, since it not only contains the answers to making your life work, but will also clear up all confusion you may have left from your childhood religion and the Bible and your schooling.

At this point you are probably in one of the following categories:

1. You have never heard of a *Course in Miracles.*

2. You have heard of it but you have not obtained a set for yourself.

3. You have obtained a set, but you have not opened it.

4. You have a set but you have only glanced at it.

5. You have started it but you quit along the way.

6. You are reading the *Course* now but not doing the lessons correctly.

7. You are reading it correctly. Bless you.

8. You are teaching the course. Thank you.

If I can get you to move up just one or two steps, I will have accomplished something. To inspire someone to read the books, and then eventually teach them, would be my highest goal.

Even though I was motivated to read the books I had considerable resistance, so I felt I could make a contribution to those of you who have had resistance. The resistance, of course, is only due to the ego, which is threatened by that much divinity. But, I assure you, transcending your resistance is worth everything because of the blessings you will receive.

My personal experience is that I would get to about lesson 280 and I would always lose the books—it was as if they would mysteriously dematerialize. (Once I mentioned this to Judith Skutch, the publisher, and what she said startled me. "Oh, that's nothing. I got to lesson such-and-such and as I was crossing the bridge over the Potomac I got out of the car and threw the books in the river.") Now you know any books that could provoke so much reaction must be incredibly powerful. These books are incredibly powerful. I certainly would not have taken three years to study them for nothing!

This book is not meant to be a substitute for the *Course*. There is no substitute for the *Course*. Nor did I change or re-interpret it in any way. Nothing should be changed or re-interpreted in this *Course*. The truth is true and every line is total enlightenment. Neither is what I left out less important than what I included. I merely extracted from the text what "leaped out at me," what seemed to me to be the essence of each chapter. I tried to give you a context, a framework, from which to get it more quickly. After reading the summary, go on to study the chapter. I felt this would be valuable, since when one starts the *Course* there is often considerable "unconsciousness" that can come up if the ego is very strong.

The first year I read the text, I could hardly stay conscious at all. I knew it was true, and yet I could not remember what I had read, nor did I feel I was able to comprehend the main points. But, I could not stop thinking about it. I kept buying new sets after losing them and beginning again. In my second year it started to make a lot of sense to me because I was less into my ego. The third year I could say with conviction "This is the ONLY thing that makes sense to me." I began to see the importance of incorporating the *Course* into all my work and teaching.

Perhaps what I included here are the parts that I myself have finally been able to integrate. Needless to say, writing this book has helped me a great deal to get it at the cellular level. It is the beginning of my commitment to teach this material, which I feel is imperative to learn if we are to have what we say we want: personal and world peace.

I suggest you use this book in the following way. For the first days, read the summary of Chapter One followed by the actual chapter in the *Course* text. Each day during that period, study one lesson in the workbook. It is important not to study more than one lesson a day. This is because too much ego could be activated if you do more. The teacher's manual that comes with the books explains this point carefully. The *Course* is brilliantly designed to offer as much as one can handle at a given time. Never jump ahead and read the later lessons before you thoroughly understand the beginning lessons.

After I got through the first eighteen lessons I noticed a major change in my consciousness. I also started having miracle experiences. Now, every time I study the *Course* I notice that my joy increases and increases.

The *Course* can be purchased at metaphysical bookstores around the country, and at churches like Unity Church and the Church of Religious Science. There are also independent booksellers, and there are study groups in every major city and many smaller towns. These study groups are helpful and serve to keep you on purpose.

What It Was Like
To Write This Book

This book was conceived, like many of my spiritual projects, after a mystical experience. I had just returned from a visit to my guru, Babaji Shri Shri 1008 Hherakan Wale Baba in the Himalayas. I had surrendered this time as much as possible, going through the "rite of passage" of the head shave, which I was to maintain for a period of nine months in the U.S. I was feeling in an altered state my first night back in America, so when somebody suggested seeing the movie *Altered States* it seemed appropriate. During the movie, however, I kept leaving my body and I felt very unusual. Suddenly I heard a loud voice in my head which said: "YOU MUST DO THE GOD TRAINING. IT IS NOT A QUESTION OF CAN YOU DO IT OR WILL YOU DO IT. IT MUST BE DONE." Extremely startled, I consented. After the movie, I wondered what on earth I had consented to. What did it mean? A year-and-a-half went by. I was very busy Rebirthing and teaching the Loving Relationships Training. Sometimes I wore a turban over my shaved head, sometimes not, as I tried to "integrate" my trip to India.

I could not forget the commitment I had made. I decided maybe it had something to do with the *Course* and that I needed to go far away from the distractions of my life and really integrate the *Course*. Finally after the Rebirthers' Jubilee I went to the travel agent and bought a ticket to Bali for Christmas. I had always dreamed of Bali; it is often called the island of the Gods. It sounded like the right place.

It was perfect, and every day there was inspiring. After twenty-two years of traveling, I found it to be the second holiest place I had ever been (next to Babaji's ashram). Everyone seemed angelic to me and I was extremely impressed that every home had a temple and that families used them daily. I never could get over it. I was in bliss every day in Bali. I spent about six weeks there in solitude. It took me that long to study my spiritual books and try to outline the text, which was groundwork for the training and which got me started on the idea for this book. After several weeks, Babaji appeared to me, calling me back to India, and I flew to New Delhi for more purification.

Another year went by and I was so busy working that I had no time to start this book. I knew I would have to go away again. It seemed necessary to purify myself, so I went on a week's cruise in the Caribbean for rest and meditation. Finally I landed in St. Martin, where I spent two weeks in solitude, putting it together. While working on this material, every day my joy increased.

My prayer for you is that every day in every way your joy will increase and that this book will play a part in it.

Enlightenment

*This book will make more sense and life will make more sense
if you understand spiritual enlightenment.*

1. Spiritual enlightenment: Having certain knowledge of the Absolute Truth.

2. Absolute Truth: Something that is always true for everyone in all space and time.

3. The Absolute Truth is: THOUGHT IS CREATIVE.

4. *Thought is creative* means: Your thoughts produce your results; positive thoughts produce positive results; negative thoughts produce negative results.

5. The way to change your results and your life, therefore, is: Change negative thoughts to positive thoughts by the process of *affirmations*. An affirmation is a positive thought that you consciously choose to immerse in your being by the process of repetition to produce a desired new result in your life.

6. Example: If you have a negative, limiting, low-self-esteem thought like "I'm not good enough," you choose to replace that thought by consciously writing and thinking the opposite: "I am good enough."

   The *Course in Miracles* would say that any negative thought is an attack on God (ego). It suggests the "Undo-Redo process":

   > "Since I was the thinker that thought I wasn't good enough, I am also the thinker that can now think I am good enough."

7. The only problem is that your subconscious thoughts are still producing results even though you are no longer thinking those thoughts consciously. We have all had negative thoughts from our birth trauma and conception trauma, for example, and these pre-verbal thoughts are still affecting us. (The most limiting negative thought we must change is "I am separate from God.")

8. Solution: Somehow these buried thoughts must come to the surface so we can change them. This we have learned to do through various spiritual purification techniques.

Purification

"Miracles are everyone's right, but purification is necessary first."
(A Course in Miracles text, p. 1)

My favorite methods of spiritual purification are:

1. Affirmations: An affirmation is a positive thought that you choose to immerse in your consciousness to produce a desired result. (See my first book *I Deserve Love* for mastery of affirmations.) Saying or writing affirmations "burns out" negativity (ego) and therefore is purifying.

2. Conscious Breathing or Rebirthing: Rebirthing is a safe and gentle breathing process that releases accumulated negativity back to and including birth. Through this process, unwanted behavior patterns are revealed and released, and the heart opens so you can receive more love, peace, abundance, and remember your Divinity. (See *Rebirthing in the New Age* and *Celebration of Breath*.)

3. Singing the Name of God; Chanting: The purpose of repeating the name of God every day is that evokes the divine presence and all divine emotions. I have received the greatest value from chanting *Om Namaha Shivai* which means "Infinite Spirit, Infinite Being and Infinite Manifestation." It also means "I bow to that part of God that destroys ignorance." Therefore, you can "burn out" your ignorant thoughts and have your positive thoughts manifest more quickly and creatively, all in one!

4. Studying the Word of God; *A Course in Miracles*, the Bible, etc.: This book is my attempt to provide a kind of study guide for the *Course in Miracles*, which I believe are the most powerful books on the planet today (along with the Bible). These books clear up the confusion, errors and misunderstandings we may have encountered in our childhood religions. They provide the answers we have been looking for, and to read them is a strong and wonderful purification.

5. Meditation, prayer and other religious practices: This is an individual choice. I personally like and benefit from Transcendental Meditation (TM) and a method of prayer I learned as a child:

Five-part prayer, daily:

1. Introduction (Reading from Scripture or metaphysical books—recommend *Course in Miracles* text, at least 8 pages.)

2. "Something I am grateful for is":

3. "Something I want to be forgiven for is (or someone I want to forgive or be forgiven by is)":

4. "Something I want to ask for is" (petition):

5. Closing (Reading from Scripture or metaphysical books—recommend *Course in Miracles* workbook lesson)

6. Surrendering to the Master (Babaji, Jesus, Saibaba, etc.): The Masters I have listed are the ones I am attuned to. You may have your own. This is rapid purification. Spiritual Masters like Moses, Buddha, Jesus and Krishna have appeared from time to time to give comfort and restore faith and righteousness in the world. Babaji has been guiding the rich and poor, scholars, seekers and saints alike with the exceptional purity and wisdom of the supreme spiritual master. You can read about him in Yogananda's book *Autobiography of a Yogi* (Chapters 33 and 34) and Leonard Orr's book *Physical Immortality* (see Appendix).

These methods of spiritual purification are not only rapid and powerful, they are, quite simply, *wonderful*.

Mind Map for Studying the Course

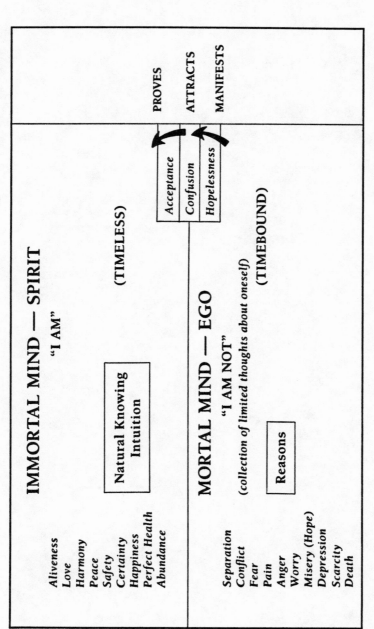

IMMORTAL MIND — SPIRIT
"I AM"
(TIMELESS)

Natural Knowing
Intuition

Aliveness
Love
Harmony
Peace
Safety
Certainty
Happiness
Perfect Health
Abundance

MORTAL MIND — EGO
"I AM NOT"
(collection of limited thoughts about oneself)
(TIMEBOUND)

Reasons

Separation
Conflict
Fear
Pain
Anger
Worry
Misery (Hope)
Depression
Scarcity
Death

Acceptance
Confusion
Hopelessness

PROVES
ATTRACTS
MANIFESTS

Chapter One

It is interesting and exciting to note that the first chapter of the Text not only talks about miracles, but also about the fact that you can abolish sickness *and death* yourself—*and* have total abundance. Jesus set the example for this, and the Text makes it very clear that there is nothing about Jesus that we could not attain. Jesus deserves our respect for his greater experience, and giving it to him will only add to our miracles.

Do you wish to have miracles and perform miracles? They are your right, but you must purify yourself first. The way to do this is to accept ATONEMENT, which means the undoing of all your wrong thinking. You must allow the Holy Spirit to do it for you. Affirm with conviction "I allow the Holy Spirit to undo all my wrong thinking." Other spiritual purification practices are listed at the end of the chapter.

The Holy Spirit is the Voice for God. The Holy Spirit is the communication link between man and God. He speaks for God and for you, being joined with both. The Holy Spirit is the highest communication medium. Have you acknowledged this? Try it.

The *Course* repeatedly states that the only thing you need to correct is your imagined separation from God. We have said before in our work in Rebirthing how this gets recreated at every conception and is part of the Conception Trauma. At conception, thinking that taking on a body made you separate from God was the number one mistake, resulting in fear, guilt, weakness, pain and (ultimately) death.

Your true reality is spirit, and spirit is that which cannot be destroyed. You cannot be destroyed if you remember that you are one with spirit. You must, of course, purify your mind by giving up the thoughts "I am separate from God" and "Death is inevitable." (See *Rebirthing in the New Age* for the subject of physical immortality.)

Chapter One reminds us there is no order of difficulty in miracles. One is no harder than another. Miracles are universal blessings of God. They are not under laws of time and are substitutes for learning what might have taken a thousand years. Miracles are natural. They are expressions of love. They express an inner awareness of Christ. They make our minds one in God and they reawaken us to the fact that spirit is truth. They are beyond the body.

The Holy Spirit is the *mechanism* for miracles. Prayer is the *medium* for miracles.

Prayer is a way offered by the Holy Spirit to reach God. Prayer is a stepping aside, a letting go, not to be confused with supplication. The secret of prayer is to forget the things you think you need. Let them go into God's hands. Prayer should be an offering, a giving up of yourself to be at one with God (love). There is nothing to ask because there is nothing left to want. The real sound should be of thanksgiving and love.

Healing the sick and raising the dead will be natural as we realize that *we* made sickness and death and therefore we can abolish them. In other words, what you have created you can uncreate. The *Course* says repeatedly that all illness is mental illness. In Rebirthing we say that all pain (and all symptoms) are the effort involved in clinging to a negative thought. This is just another way of saying that all illness is mental illness. (See *Celebration of Breath* for healing symptoms by healing the mind.)

Chapter One reminds us to become as little children. We must remember God is our Father and we must recognize our complete dependence on him. All pleasure comes from doing God's will, and God's will for you is perfect happiness. You may not believe this if your life is miserable. You may believe God is out to get you. You must remind yourself, however, that God did not create your misery, you did. You did it with your own negative thoughts (ego). If you have trouble in this area, meditate on the following line from the *Course*: "You will attack what doesn't satisfy you to avoid seeing that you created it."

Another important thought is "Only you can deprive yourself of anything." Chapter One states that deprivation is of the ego. The natural result of following in Christ's footsteps is abundance. Those who are Christ-like and expressing miracles are showing that they have given up deprivation and favor abundance.

You deserve miracles and abundance and you can create them. You were created to create the good, the beautiful and the holy. If you aren't

2

creating that, your thoughts need purifying. For help in purifying your thoughts I recommend:

1. *A Course in Miracles* (ask at a Unity church or order from Life Unlimited)

2. *Rebirthing* (Read *Rebirthing in the New Age* and *Celebration of Breath*)

3. *The Loving Relationships Training* (read *Loving Relationships,* call (203) 354-8509)

4. All of my books (and the books recommended in my books)

5. *Meditation/Prayer/Surrendering to Jesus and Babaji* (for information on Babaji, read *Autobiography of a Yogi,* Chapters 33 and 34, plus *Physical Immortality* by Leonard Orr)

Examples of Applications for Chapter One

1. Since one miracle is no harder than another, it is no harder to heal cancer or poor eyesight or even blindness than it is to heal a cut or a common cold.

2. Since I am not separate from God, I am therefore one with God; I can be anything, do anything and have anything.

3. Since deprivation is of the ego, which is a collection of negative thoughts I have had about myself, I can change to overflowing abundance by changing my negative thoughts to positive affirmations.

4. Since it is necessary to purify the mind before being entitled to miracles, I am happy that there are now simple ways like Rebirthing and affirmations to help me do it.

5. Since I am not really separate from God, I am not separate from anything. This means that I can be with anyone at the speed of thought. Telepathy is natural.

On a separate piece of paper, make a list of your own applications.

During the ten days you are studying Chapter One in the Text, learn one lesson a day in the workbook, summarizing what you learned in this space.

Day 1:＿＿＿＿＿＿＿＿＿＿＿＿＿＿＿＿＿＿＿＿＿＿＿＿＿

Day 2:＿＿＿＿＿＿＿＿＿＿＿＿＿＿＿＿＿＿＿＿＿＿＿＿＿

Day 3:＿＿＿＿＿＿＿＿＿＿＿＿＿＿＿＿＿＿＿＿＿＿＿＿＿

Day 4:_____

Day 5:_____

Day 6:_____

Day 7:_____

Day 8:_____

Day 9:_____

Day 10:_____

Chapter Two

You were created perfect. God extended Himself to you, and you are like Him and therefore creative. You cannot lose this ability to create. You were created perfect with no emptiness.

When you believe that there is some lack of emptiness in you, and you fill this with your own ideas, this is where you get in trouble! You mistakenly think you can change what God created by your own mind. Then you distort things, which leads to separation, a detour into fear. This distortion, called the ego (a collection of negative, limiting thoughts one has about oneself), does not even exist. It is not real. You made it up. It is an illusion. The ego is insane. The ego is fear. All fear is reducible to this: thinking you have the ability to usurp the power of God.

When you are afraid of anything you are acknowledging its power to hurt you. *Deny* that error can hurt you! This would be correct thinking. You cannot perform miracles while beset with doubt and fear. You must give up the defense mechanisms of fear and attack. (The best defense is no defense. Being one with God is the only defense you would ever need. God is the only safety there is.) It is safe to have miracles. God asks you to perform miracles. Ask Jesus which miracles to perform.

Acknowledge that what you have been doing is using defense against the atonement. This maintains the separation and results in a need to defend the body. Keeping out God makes you weak. Fear, guilt, pain and misery are ways we keep out God. This weakens us so much that we think we need protection, which is not the truth.

Defenses make you weak because by their very existence they imply that you are weak. Since what you fear, you attract, the defense will

only make you more susceptible. It is therefore more dangerous.
Chapter Two gives the formula for healing very clearly.

The Principle is the Atonment.
The means is the miracle.
The result is total healing.

All healing is the release from fear. All illness is mental illness (i.e. sickness is not right-mindedness). Remedies are forms of magic. They are not needed; they simply give form to the patient's wishes. (The physician is actually the mind of the patient!) However, if an illness has a very strong hold over someone, it is appropriate to compromise, since not taking medicine may produce more fear and further weaken the person.

God wants you to become a miracle worker. The function of a miracle worker is to realize that correction always belongs at the thought level. However, if the person is afraid to use the mind to heal, do not force it. The miracle worker's purpose is to restore a person to his right-mindedness. You, the miracle worker, have to be in your right mind. Here is suggested mind preparation: "I am here to be truly helpful. I am here to represent the Holy Spirit. I will be directed so that I don't have to worry. I will be healed as I let Him teach me how to heal."

Miracles come from thoughts. Fear comes from thoughts. One must give up fear in order to have and perform miracles. The correction of fear is our own responsibility. We must not ask for release from fear, as that implies it is somebody else's responsibility. Ask instead for help in dealing with the conditions that brought about our fear. *This has to do with thinking you are separate from God.* Whenever you are afraid, it comes from a misconception. Fear is from lack of love. The only remedy for lack of love is perfect love. Perfect love is the Atonement. Conflict is just an expression of fear and only your mind can produce fear and conflict. Place what you think under the guidance of the Holy Spirit, as this immediately connects you to the truth.

The last judgment is not punishment, but right evaluation. It is reaping the results of your thinking. When you think right you will get good results, so that the last judgment will not be the end, but the doorway to life.

Examples of Applications for Chapter Two

1. I remember that I was created perfect and still am. Any of the things that seem to me imperfect are really lies, and I confess I made them up to usurp the power of God. I had the notion that, if I made myself less than perfect, it proved I was more powerful. This is insanity.

2. I was wrong when I thought putting walls around me would make me strong. I was wrong when I thought I needed protection. I was wrong when I added fear, guilt and pain as defenses against God. These things only made me weaker and in need of more protection, which made me still weaker. Defenses attract attack, so I now remain totally open and vulnerable to be safer. Since I am one with God I have all the safety I need.

3. I can heal myself totally by remembering I am one with God and by allowing all my wrong thinking to be undone and accepting the miracle. In order to heal myself I can aid the situation by locating the negative thought (ego) causing the condition and by letting it go.

4. I can also honor my fears and, until I learn to heal myself totally using only my mind, it is OK to use other forms of healing (such as pills) so that my fear will not be too great. I am, however, committed to learning how to heal myself totally with my mind alone. And I am ultimately committed to learning how to prevent disease altogether.

5. I can assist others to heal themselves by helping them see that correction begins by changing their thoughts. I can teach them affirmations. I always remember to honor their fear and not push them.

6. I do not expect anyone else to take away my fears. I take responsibility for making them up. In general, I made them up because I thought I was separate from God. This was a mistake. I forgive myself for thinking I was separate from God. I am forgiven.

7. I am perfect, God-like. This is not blasphemy. I forgive whoever taught me that. It is time to start living my perfection.

On a separate piece of paper, make a list of your own applications.

*D*uring the ten days you are studying Chapter Two
in the Text, learn one lesson a day in the workbook,
summarizing what you learned in this space.

Day 11:_____

Day 12:_____

Day 13:_____

Day 14:_____

Day 15:_____

Day 16:_____

Day 17:_____

Day 18:_____

Day 19:_____

Day 20:_____

Chapter Three

Chapter three begins by explaining that one reason people fear God is because they misunderstand the Crucifixion and Resurrection. If you focus on the Crucifixion wrongly, you might assume that God encouraged a son to suffer. This is a projection and makes people fear God. God does not believe in retribution and Jesus was not punished because man was bad. Sacrifice is completely unknown to God. The Resurrection established the Atonement and demonstrated that nothing can destroy truth. It also demonstrated that good can withstand any form of evil.

We must let go of our own distortions. To do this we need to separate perception from knowledge. To know is to be certain. Knowledge is timeless. Certainty is strength. Certainty is of God. Perception, however, is temporary, subject to fear. It involves interpretation and is not consistent. It depends on time. Knowing is the affirmation of truth, beyond all perception. The Bible tells you to know yourself and be certain. To *recognize* means "to know again." God is not a stranger to his Children and they are not strangers to each other. All your difficulty stems from the fact that you do not recognize yourself, your sisters and brothers, or God. It is because you have made people strangers that you attack them. You make them strangers by misperceiving them. The choice to judge rather than to know causes loss of peace, because judgement always involves rejection.

Be clear that the ego was not created. It was *made up.* There is a difference between creating and making something up. When you make up something, you do so out of a perceived sense of lack of need, which implies that you believe in separation. At this point the *Course* makes

13

the bold statement that you are so confused between your real creation and what you made up that it is impossible to know *anything*. In other words, our ego is so far off track that we have buried the natural knowing. Knowledge is stable. The fact that we are so unstable proves we disagree with God's creation. This is our sin. We think we can make what is perfect imperfect.

The ego was made by us, an aspect of the separated self. This separated mind is inevitably confused. By misusing the mind, for example, you have interpreted the body to be yourself. You are not your body. With this misperception you made the spirit nearly inaccessible, and therefore you perceive spirit as a threat. *Truth cannot deal with errors that you cherish.*

The *Course* makes it plain that your mind can return to its proper function only when you place it in service to spirit. By uniting your will with the Creator, you will remember spirit. But no one can unite your will with God's for you. You must choose. The Chosen Ones are the ones who chose right sooner. Pray on this. Forgiveness is the healing of the perception of separation, therefore the only meaningful prayer is for forgiveness. Those who have been forgiven have everything.

Ultimately communion, not prayer, is the natural state of those who know.

The root of all evil is what the *Course* calls the authority problem. This is when you believe that you are the author of yourself and perceive others are fighting for your authorship. If you choose to separate yourself from your real author, God (by thinking God is outside of you somewhere else), then you believe your creating was *anonymous*. This leaves you in uncertainty whether you exist at all. Fear and lack of peace come from denial of authorship.

You must remember that nothing is made by you without power. The mind can make the belief in separation very real and very frightening. This belief (separation-ego) *is* the devil. It is powerful, active, destructive and in opposition to God. You made it. Confess that you made it.

Examples of Applications for Chapter Three

1. I can finally give up my fear of God's punishment and relax. I was wrong when I thought God punished people. I forgive those who taught me this and I forgive myself for believing it.

2. Since God's will for me is only perfect happiness, I am no longer afraid of God's will. (When bad things happened, that was not God's will for me, it was the creation of my own impure subconscious mind.) God's will brings me everything I want. God's will and my will are one now. So be it.

3. From now on, in every brother I see God. I recognize myself in him. I recognize God in him. I do not wish to attack myself or God, therefore I do not attack my brother. Since I know my brother and my brother knows me, we are in a loving relationship. There is no need to play games of "strangers."

4. I pray for forgiveness regarding the distortions I have made that kept spirit out. I choose not to maintain these distortions that cause separation. I do not want this error any longer. "I am one with spirit, one with joy, one with life and one with abundance and all that God is."

5. "I know what I am and I accept my own inheritance."

6. Whenever I am tempted by the devil (my own ego) I do what Jesus did, saying "Get thee behind me, Satan" which means "Get away, negative thoughts, I will not indulge in you or believe in you. I relinquish you. My mind is God's mind."

7. In my Rebirthing sessions, I remember there is no separation between me and my Rebirther and me and God. Therefore it is totally safe. While breathing I remind myself I can change any negative thought that comes up by breathing it out and saying the opposite as an affirmation. Therefore there is no need to fear being stuck or in danger.

On a separate piece of paper, make a list of your own applications.

During the ten days you are studying Chapter Three in the Text, learn one lesson a day in the workbook, summarizing what you learned in this space.

Day 21: _____

Day 22: _____

Day 23: _____

Day 24: _____

Day 25: _____

Day 26: _____

Day 27: _____

Day 28: _____

Day 29: _____

Day 30: _____

Chapter Four

In each second you have a choice; the spirit or the ego. You can speak from either as you choose. But when you speak from the ego, you are disclaiming knowledge and dis-spiriting yourself. Don't make the mistake of clinging to the old rugged cross. It is time to change.

Before we can change we have to handle fear of change. In Rebirthing we talk about people fearing change because the first change caused pain (i.e. going from a liquid environment to an atmospheric environment and getting slapped in order to breathe). But going even further back, the *Course* reminds us that separation was our first experience of change; therefore we fear change will move us toward further separation.

We must correct these fears because they are in opposition to God. The ego and God are not in communication. Therefore we are not communicating with God when we are into the ego (negative, limiting thoughts). The ego needs to be taught, but this is frightening because it leads to the relinquishment of the ego. The *Course* tells you how to do it gently: Renounce the role of the ego and open your thoughts to Jesus. The ego is afraid of the joy of the spirit, because once you have experienced this joy, you will never go back—you will withdraw from the ego.

Incidentally, don't bother trying to figure out why you made the ego and separated. Just let go. Only the ego wants to study itself. The ego's existence depends on your continuing belief in separation. The reward the ego promises is *temporary* existence (death). (You secretly hate the self you made. *Therefore you cannot believe that God loves you,* and you think you must die.)

The Holy Spirit cannot penetrate walls you've made. Truth cannot deal with errors that you want. This is because the Holy Spirit will not add to your fear. It is, however, a constant reminder that there is available to you an existence so different from what the ego offers that you will never want to bury it again. Love will enter immediately if you truly want it. In moments of temptation use the following prayer as your declaration of independence:

"The Kingdom is perfectly united and perfectly protected; and the ego will not prevail against it." Amen.

Misery is associated with the ego. Joy is associated with the spirit. Whenever you are not feeling joyous, you have chosen wrongly. Your thoughts are "off." This need not be! You are deprived of nothing except by your own decision. When you feel guilty, your ego is in command. This need not be! Uniting with Christ shines the ego away. (The Second Coming means the end of the ego's rule.)

The ego will try to disrupt communication because it believes your existence is defined by separation. Being is a state where the mind is in communication with everything that is real. God created beings who have everything individually, but who want to share it to increase their joy. Nothing real can be increased except by sharing. That is why God created you.

Examples of Applications for Chapter Four

1. I can change without pain and separation. The more I change by letting go of the ego, the safer I am. The more I change, the more I am united, and therefore the safer I am. It is safe to change completely.

2. I do not let my ego keep me from the joy I deserve. When I feel fear around joy it is not because joy is fearful. It is just my ego trying to keep me away from that joy. I will not run from the joy, having judged it as fearful. I will go toward joy, not letting my ego prevail. I trust that joy is safe.

3. I will not let the ego convince me that death and temporary existence are the right goals and results. I know that spirit is eternal and that God loves me, therefore I deserve eternality. I no longer hate myself, therefore I accept what the spirit offers: permanence.

4. I choose to let go of fear. I can do this by changing the thoughts I have that produce the fear; I can also breathe out fear on the exhale.

5. When I am not feeling joyous, I remember I have chosen wrongly. I can clear this by asking myself "What have I thought that God would *not* have thought? What have I thought that God would have me think?

6. Whenever I feel upset I can command "This need not be." I can remind myself that I am not "stuck with it." I am never stuck with any situation. I can self-correct and create a better situation.

7. Whenever I am tempted to fight or be witness to an argument, I remind myself that it is my ego wanting to disrupt communication and keep me separate. I can change this situation with a higher thought.

On a separate piece of paper, make a list of your own applications.

*During the ten days you are studying Chapter Four
in the Text, learn one lesson a day in the workbook,
summarizing what you learned in this space.*

Day 31: _____

Day 32: _____

Day 33: _____

Day 34: _____

Day 35: _____

Day 36: _____

Day 37: _____

Day 38: _____

Day 39: _____

Day 40: _____

Chapter Five

To heal is to make happy. You have had many opportunities to gladden yourself, but you have refused them.

Jesus came to bring the Holy Spirit to you, but only at your invitation does he enter. By inviting the Holy Spirit, you receive the mind of the Atonement. When you choose the Holy Spirit, you choose God. God is not in you. You are part of God.

When you chose to leave God and made the ego, communication was broken because you made another voice. The Voice of the Holy Spirit is quiet because it speaks of peace. It does not demand, command, overcome. It merely reminds. (The voice of the ego is loud and demanding, tempting you to pain, guilt, fear and suffering. When you aré tempted by it, call on the Holy Spirit.)

Another term for separation is "split mind." You made the ego and weakened ourself, but if you allow, the Holy Spirit will use it as a teaching device to bring you back home to God.

Jesus calls you to teach what you have learned. Teaching will heal you further because it is the sharing of ideas, and to share ideas is to strengthen them. Thoughts increase by giving them away. The decision to share thoughts is their purification. Since the Voice of the Holy Spirit is still weak within you, you must share it to increase its strength. Besides, you cannot find your way to God without taking others with you.

Whenever you respond to your ego, you will experience guilt and fear punishment. You think you detached yourself from God, therefore you believe you are attacking God. Guilt shows that you want to think apart from God and that you believe you can. If you identify with the ego and guilt, retaliation follows, because the ego believes that punishing itself will mitigate the punishment of God. Illness is a way the ego acts this out. Guilt is always disruptive. It is a sure sign that your thinking is unnatural. Guilt is not only not of God, it is an attack on God.

The ego will convince you that you cannot escape from it. But you can and must escape! The Holy Spirit can set you free, but the ego will oppose it every second. Even the Bible will be frightening to the ego, which will interpret it fearfully. (Example: The wicked shall perish is really the wicked shall be *undone*.)

The ego offers limited existence	*God offers continuity and eternity*
The ego offers guilt	*God offers joy*
The ego offers viciousness	*God offers love*
The ego offers pain	*God offers peace*

The last-ditch defense of the ego is excluding yourself from the Atonement. If you side with separation, you do not want to be healed! Do you really believe you can make a voice that drowns out God's? Do you really believe you can plan your safety better than He can? Remember the ego is insane. You cannot cancel out your errors alone. They will not disappear without the Atonement.

Remember, when you are not wholly joyous, you have chosen wrongly. You must choose again. Choose a new thought!

Examples of Applications for Chapter Five

1. Only good will come to me by inviting the Holy Spirit, therefore I no longer deny myself this opportunity to become happy. I invite it now.

2. When I am tempted by the voice of the ego and start to suffer, I remember to resist this temptation through my spiritual practices of praying, chanting, rebirthing, affirming, and reading the *Course*. I do not wait until the suffering gets a hold on me.

3. I turn over my ego to the Holy Spirit to be used as a communication and teaching device.

4. When I am most resisting help is when I need help the most. The affirmations I resist the most are the ones I need the most. I remember this and rise above the resistance to seek help. I seek help.

5. When I do not feel good and if I am not joyous, I realize I have chosen wrongly. I get released by the Undo-Redo process:
   I must have decided wrongly because I am not at peace.
   I made the decision myself, but I can also decide otherwise.
   I want to decide otherwise, because I want to be at peace.
   I do not feel guilty because the Holy Spirit will undo all the consequences of my wrong decision if I will allow it.
   I chose to allow it to decide for God for me.

6. Since I was the thinker that thought _____
   I am also the thinker that can now think _____

7. I will not attack God by hanging on to guilt. I focus on innocence. Ways I can experience my innocence are:_____
   _____

8. The more I give up the guilt the healthier I'll be, because I won't use the making of illness as a way to punish myself.

9. I am willing to share my enlightenment with others by telling them of the opportunities available (seminars, rebirthing, books, the *Course*). I talk about it as much as possible.

On a separate piece of paper, make a list of your own applications.

*During the ten days you are studying Chapter Five
in the Text, learn one lesson a day in the workbook,
summarizing what you learned in this space.*

Day 41: _____

Day 42: _____

Day 43: _____

Day 44: _____

Day 45: _____

Day 46: _____

Day 47: _____

Day 48: _____

Day 49: _____

Day 50: _____

Chapter Six

The Crucifixion was not a form of punishment, but an extreme example of a teaching device. To those who understand it, it is a release from fear. You have been reacting for years as if you were being crucified. Anger cannot occur unless you believe you have been attacked, that your counter-attack is justified, and that you are not responsible in any way. Anger always involves projection and separation. You cannot be attacked, attack has no justification, and you *are* responsible.

The Crucifixion was intended to teach that it is not necessary to perceive any form of assault as persecution, because you cannot be persecuted. If you respond with anger, you are equating yourself with the destructible and regarding yourself insanely. If you react as if you are persecuted you are teaching persecution, because what you believe, you teach.

Your Resurrection is your Reawakening.

Jesus is the model for Rebirth. If you accept him as a model, you are one of his disciples. He has chosen to save disciples pain in all respects. *You are wise to follow him, unwise not to follow him.* If you interpret the Crucifixion any other way, you are using it as a weapon. It is really a call for peace. But even the Apostles misunderstood. They spoke of the wrath of God and misquoted Jesus as having said "I am come not to bring peace but a sword." That was their projection out of fear.

The separation was, and is, disassociation. Its defense becomes projection, because what you project you disown, not believing it is yours. You assume you are different from the one you are judging, and therefore you exclude yourself. But projection will always hurt you. It makes you seem even more separate. The alternative to projection is *extension.* The Holy Spirit sees you as perfect, recognizes perfection in others and strengthens it in all; this arouses love. The only safety lies in extending the Holy Spirit. The gentleness will enable you to see your own mind as harmless.

The following will help you to see how insane the ego is, how it is an expert in confusion and why it is the devil:

> You made the ego without love and so it does not love you. Then you believe you are without love. The Kingdom is love, but the ego makes you believe you are separate from that love. The ego believes that the part of the mind that made it is against it and this is justification for attacking it. It turns to the body and uses the body to conspire against your mind, trying to convince you that the body is more real than the mind.
>
> This war is clearly insane. Perhaps you think you'll get out of this mess through death and last forever through death. Nothing is accomplished through death.

Everything is accomplished through life. If you share the mind of Christ, you can overcome death as He did. The Holy Spirit will teach you the right approach. Do only this:

1. Return your whole mind to God, because it has never actually left. The separation never really occurred. The ego cannot prevail against this because it is a statement that the ego never occurred.

2. Your salvation lies in teaching the exact opposite of everything the ego believes.

3. To have all, give all. Turn your body over to be used as a communication device. Give it to the Holy Spirit for its use. Communication when shared becomes communion. Undo the "getting" concept. Having rests on giving.

4. Teach peace to learn it. Peace of mind is not possible if you accept two thought systems. If a lie is at the center of a thought system (as it is with the ego, imagining separation) only deception can come from it. If you teach both, you are teaching conflict and learning conflict. Allow the Holy Spirit to decide for God for you. Teach only peace. The role of a good teacher is to strengthen and increase motivation for change. Be vigilant only for God in order to change.

   Step 1: Beginning thought reversal
   Step 2: Identification of what is more desirable

Step 3: The ultimate choice: vigilance against conflict and relinquishing everything to the Holy Spirit.
*Only the Holy Spirit can resolve conflict because only the Holy Spirit
is free of conflict.*

Examples of Applications for Chapter Six

1. No one can hurt me or attack me but myself. I forgive myself for making attack real when it is not.

2. Instead of expressing or repressing anger, I will locate and change the thoughts causing my anger. I will not lower my vibration to that of anger because it is destructive to my energy body.

3. I wish to follow the example of Jesus because He leads me out of pain.

4. I forgive everyone who misinterpreted the Bible through the ego and those who confused me. I forgive myself for "buying into" this confusion.

5. I forgive myself for projecting my thoughts onto others. I am for-given by them. I now choose to expend love rather than project; I also remember that all blame is off the track.

6. I am no longer concerned about getting. I am committed to giving all that I can. This is the way to be saved.

7. I choose peace over conflict. I am careful not to create conflict, add to it or support it in my space.

8. I am willing to change. I am now an inspiration to others to change.

9. I always reach for the highest, most spiritual thoughts. I identify with that which is good for me. Heaven is a decision I am willing to make now.

10. I am willing to promote peace, spread and teach peace. I give up all conflict in myself so that I am becoming peace of mind myself.

On a separate piece of paper, make a list of your own applications.

D*uring the ten days you are studying Chapter Six*
in the Text, learn one lesson a day in the workbook,
summarizing what you learned in this space.

Day 51: Review Lessons 1 to 5 _____

Day 52: Review Lessons 6 to 10 _____

Day 53: Review Lessons 11 to 15 _____

Day 54: Review Lessons 16 to 20_____

Day 55: Review Lessons 21 to 25_____

Day 56: Review Lessons 26 to 30_____

Day 57: Review Lessons 31 to 35_____

Day 58: Review Lessons 36 to 40 _____

Day 59: Review Lessons 41 to 45 _____

Day 60: Review Lessons 46 to 50 _____

Chapter Seven

Consider the Kingdom that you have made:

Is it worthy to be the home of the Son of God?

Does it protect your peace and shine love on you?

Does it keep your heart untouched by fear?

Does it allow you to give always without a sense of loss?

Does it teach you giving is joy?

You are outside the real Kingdom. You cannot be happy in this environment because:

The ego is competitive rather than loving.

The ego perceives itself at war.

The ego believes it can oppose the Will of God and offer you its own will.

The ego has induced a sense of danger in you.

The ego tries to teach you the body does not need the mind and is self-sufficient. (The body in service to the ego can hurt other bodies.)

The ego convinces you that healing is actually harmful.

The ego opposes all appreciation, all recognition, all sane perception, all knowledge. It sees them as a total threat.

The ego's picture of you is deprived, unloving and weak.

The ego tries to preserve conflict.

The ego uses projection to trick you into thinking *you* don't have the problem, the other person has the problem.

The ego believes it can attack God.

The ego is selfishness.

The ego blocks your joy.

The ego's reasoning carried to conclusion is total confusion about everything.

This is the kingdom you have made. Judge its worth.

You do not want it. Are you ready to trade it in for the true Kingdom of the Heavenly Father?

The gifts of the True Kingdom are many.

Start with perfect love.

There is only certainty.

All power is yours and you are the way, the truth and the life.

You recognize other people as equals.

You are at peace.

You have everything and there is no competition.

Everything is unified and healed.

There is no lack.

There is only joy.

You have God's blessing forever and you share that.

You have abundance and you share that.

Self-fullness is the result.

Grace is the natural state.

There is no strain.

You are happy because you are with God and this is where you belong.

To have this Kingdom, you must dispel the ego. You can do this by withdrawing belief in it. You must not project the responsibility for your belief in it onto anyone else.

The Kingdom cannot be found alone. If you only look at yourself, you cannot find yourself. With your brother you are learning what you are. When you meet anyone, remember it is a holy encounter.

Examples of Applications for Chapter Seven

1. I have evaluated the Kingdom I have made in terms of results and have seen clearly that it does not work. It brings me misery and I see it is not the real truth.

2. I confess that I have been confused and completely off track. I confess that I have resisted healing. I confess that I have been completely stuck in the ego.

3. I confess that I have created conflict, indulged in arguing and contributed to war. My worst sin has been trying to oppose the will of God by trying to make myself less than perfect.

4. *I am willing for my ego to fail so I can experience the success of God.*

5. I no longer blame others. I take total responsibility for what I have made. I now give over all my abilities to be used properly by the Holy Spirit.

6. I would rather win love than arguments. I choose peace. I see no danger in any of my brothers.

7. I turn over all my relationships to the Holy Spirit to be made holy for serving God and sharing the light.

8. I commit my most intimate relationships to the Holy Spirit to be made holy for serving God and sharing the light.

9. I now focus all my attention on God's Kingdom so that I can be in heaven consciousness and share it. Since heaven is the realm of perfect ideas, I can be in heaven now. I forgive myself for thinking I had to die in order to be in heaven.

10. I chose the joy of God instead of pain.

On a separate piece of paper, make a list of your own applications.

*During the ten days you are studying Chapter Seven
in the Text, learn one lesson a day in the workbook,
summarizing what you learned in this space.*

Day 61: _____

Day 62: _____

Day 63: _____

Day 64: _____

Day 65: _____

Day 66: _____

Day 67: _____

Day 68: _____

Day 69: _____

Day 70: _____

SUMMARY OF

Chapter Eight

Are you satisfied with what your learning has brought you? If you want a different outcome, a change in the curriculum is obviously necessary. The curriculum of the Atonement is the opposite of the curriculum you have established for yourself.

> The ego does not even know what it is trying to teach. It is trying to teach you what you are without knowing what you are. It has never given you a sensible answer to anything. It tries to teach you that you want to oppose God's will.

The Holy Spirit's teaching takes you one direction and has only one goal. The direction is freedom, the goal is God.

The only joy and peace that can be fully known is to fulfill the will of God perfectly. To wish for something else will block it; that is why it requires total willingness on your part.

Jesus meant it literally when he said, "I am with you always." Jesus can tell you what to do, but you must first collaborate by believing he knows what to do. (The world despises and rejects Jesus because the world is the belief that love is impossible.) Jesus is with you and you are accepting God. Separation is overcome by *union*. Healing reflects the will of you and God.

The major part of this chapter has to do with the body, illness and healing. By equating yourself with a body, you will always experience depression, because the ego separates through the body. This fosters illness. To the ego, the body is a weapon and it teaches you to attack with it. The body, then, is not the source of its own health. *The ego has a profound investment in sickness.* A sick body, however, makes no sense. It comes from two premises:

1. That the body is intended for attack.

2. That you *are* the body, and so you should attack.

Sickness is a way of attacking yourself. You create sickness with your own negative thoughts. It is a way of demonstrating you can be hurt and that you need external help (such as endless prescriptions with catastrophic outcomes). All forms of sickness and even death are physical expressions of fear of awakening. All forms of sickness are signs that the mind is split. Sickness is not of the body, but of the mind. All illness is mental illness.

When you are sick, do not ask the Holy Spirit to heal the body. Ask rather that it teach you the right perception of the body.

Health is the natural state of everything when interpretation is left to the Holy Spirit. Health is the result of giving up all attempts to use the body lovelessly. Healing involves replacing fear with love.

At night, place your rest under the care of your true teacher, the Holy Spirit.

Examples of Applications for Chapter Eight

1. I am willing to admit that everything I taught myself was distorted because there was a lie at the core. I confess that because I thought I was separate I did not know who I was.

2. I choose the direction of freedom and I am totally willing to fulfill the will of God.

3. I trust in and appreciate my elder brother Jesus and I am willing to collaborate with him. I join with him now.

4. I am not my body. I forgive myself for using my body to attack others. I forgive myself for attacking myself.

5. I no longer make up disease in order to punish myself.

6. I am able to heal myself completely because anything I made up I can unmake with the same power. Example: The negative thought I had that caused this condition is: _____

   _____

   The affirmation I need to heal this condition is: _____

   _____

7. I take full responsibility for the fact that I made up pain, discomfort, sickness, and even death with my own mind.

8. I ask to be taught right perception of the body.

9. I love myself and I love my body. I treat it like a temple. I love it as much as God loves the earth, which is immortal. I forgive myself for having had the thought that death is inevitable. Since I am really one with the spirit, which cannot be destroyed, then I am indestructible.

On a separate piece of paper, make a list of your own applications.

D*uring the ten days you are studying Chapter Eight*
in the Text, learn one lesson a day in the workbook,
summarizing what you learned in this space.

Day 71: _____

Day 72: _____

Day 73: _____

Day 74: _____

Day 75: _____

Day 76: _____

Day 77: _____

Day 78: _____

Day 79: _____

Day 80: _____

Chapter Nine

*Y*ou do not realize the enormous waste of energy you spend in denying the truth (not accepting the Atonement). You have devoted your mind to what you don't want. If your mind believes that its will is different from God, it can only decide that there is no God, or that God's will is to be feared. (The former is the atheist. This insane decision will induce panic because the atheist believes he is alone. The latter is the martyr. This insane decision will induce panic because the martyr believes God is crucifying him.)

You may insist that the Holy Spirit does not answer you. But you keep asking the ego, which cannot possibly give anything. The ego cannot ask the Holy Spirit for anything because there is a complete communication failure between them. Besides, you are afraid of receiving what you really want.

At this point the *Course* clearly covers the issue of answering prayer. Pay attention if you are one of those who feels his prayers were not answered. It explains thus: Suppose you ask the Holy Spirit for something but you are still afraid of it. If this is so, attainment of it would be too scary, and that is not what you want. The Holy Spirit will never add to your fear. Answers are gifts waiting for you—until you work out your fear. (Suppose you asked for a physical healing but the threat to your belief system would be more frightening than your disease.)

As to healing others, you must accept them as they are and see them healed and sane. All others are a part of you. If you perceive their errors and make them real, you are accepting yours as real. Then you will believe that you have to undo what you have made in order to be

49

forgiven. The ego will tell you it is right to point out and correct errors in others. But when you are correcting someone you are making him wrong. *Even though his ego is always wrong, he is right.* Tell him this telepathically. Look behind the error from the beginning. The ego wants you to see the error and make it real. Jesus did not make real the unreal and then destroy it. That is not how he healed.

An unhealed healer is one who is trying to give what he has not received. He is following the ego's plan. For example, theologians may be teaching condemnation and fearful solutions. Projecting on God, they make Him appear retaliative and fear his retribution. (But can you find light by acknowledging darkness?) The psychotherapist may interpret the ego's symbols and try to prove they are real. (But can you find light by analyzing darkness?)

The Holy Spirit is the only real therapist. He will tell you what to do to help anyone. (I recommend the sequel to the *Course,* called *Psychotherapy: Purpose, Process and Practice.* This, I feel, is a must for all Rebirthers.)

It is not blasphemy, nor grandiosity, nor arrogance, to be like God.

There is a big difference between grandiosity and grandeur. Because you believe you are little, you over-compensate and counteract with grandiosity, which is always a cover for despair. Competitiveness is the essence of grandiosity. (In the LRT we say that egotism is different from self-esteem. Egotism is trying to prove you are OK after you've fallen into hating yourself.) You made grandiosity and you are afraid of it because it is a form of attack. But grandeur is of God, who created it out of love.

Your grandeur is your abundance. Bless it. To accept yourself as God created you cannot be arrogance. To accept littleness is arrogant, because it means you believe your evaluation of yourself is truer than God's. With all the grandeur of God in you, you have chosen to be little and lament it. Every minute and every second you are given a chance to save yourself. You won't be at peace until you accept the Atonement and all its grandeur.

Examples of Applications for Chapter Nine

1. I am neither alone, nor at the effect of something outside of me that will "get" me. God is real and available and always loves me. I am one with God.

2. When my prayers appear to be unanswered, I am blocking. Either 1) I have asked for something that I am too afraid to receive, or 2) I am giving a double message and have a negative sabotaging thought in my subconscious that keeps me from receiving, or 3) I may not want to receive because my need to stay angry for not receiving is stronger than my desire to have.

3. In healing my body, the first thing I do is pray for release of fear of healing. It is safe to be without this defense mechanism. I am safer the healthier I am. I am safe with all the aliveness and energy I will receive as I give up this condition.

4. I believe in my sisters and brothers and I accept them, side with them and value them. When brothers or sisters behave insanely, I see them as sane and do not make their errors real. I see behind them. I see them as healed. I see them as well.

5. I devote my life to healing myself completely. (As a Rebirther, for example, I frequently get rebirthed by another Rebirther. As a therapist, I am also clearing myself with a professional I respect.)

6. I accept my grandeur with confidence and maintain this self-esteem always. God is incomplete without me. I am immensely valuable.

7. In this Holy Instant I completely accept the Atonement for myself.

On a separate piece of paper, make a list of your own applications.

During the ten days you are studying Chapter Nine
in the Text, learn one lesson a day in the workbook,
summarizing what you learned in this space.

Day 81: Review Lessons 61 and 62 _____

Day 82: Review Lessons 63 and 64 _____

Day 83: Review Lessons 65 and 66 _____

Day 84: Review Lessons 67 and 68_____

Day 85: Review Lessons 69 and 70_____

Day 86: Review Lessons 71 and 72_____

Day 87: Review Lessons 73 and 74_____

Day 88: Review Lessons 75 and 76_____

Day 89: Review Lessons 77 and 78_____

Day 90: Review Lessons 79 and 80_____

Chapter Ten

God gave you the power to create for yourself so you would be like Him. You dream you are in exile, but you are perfectly capable of awakening to reality. Reality is that you are at home in God. Nothing that happens to you is caused by any actors outside yourself. The main point is that you have forgotten. You decided against your true reality, attacked yourself, hated what you think you are, and then suffered. Sickness is one of the ways you attack your self.

The *Course* is very clear as it states that sickness is idolatry because it is the belief that power can be taken away from you. When you do not value yourself you become sick. Sickness was made by you as a replacement for God. However you *cannot* replace God, so sickness is an illusion. God created you perfect. If you believe you can be sick, you have made up other gods before Him. The god of sickness that you made is a symbol of deciding against God. You are afraid because you know this god cannot be reconciled with God's will.

To deny God is to deny your own identity. (The wages of sin, in this case *is* death. Allegiance to the denial of God is the ego's religion.)
Sickness and death are an attack on God.

Blasphemy means you are not willing to know yourself or you are willing to *not* know yourself. If God knows His children to be wholly sinless, it is blasphemous to perceive yourself or others as guilty. If God knows you as wholly without pain, it is blasphemous to perceive suffering anywhere. If God knows you as wholly joyous, it is blasphemous to feel depressed. *Your Father created you wholly without pain and suffering of any kind. If you deny Him, you bring sin, pain and suffering into your mind.* (God will not interfere with you because then you would not be free.)

When another appears to be sick, do not side with the sickness, even if he or she believes it strongly, or you will be worshipping the same idol. To believe that a child of God can be sick is to believe that part of God can suffer. When people are sick, it is because they don't know they have peace for the asking. Accept God in them, which will acknowledge the love of God they have forgotten. Accept peace in them. You can weaken their belief in sickness because the power of your mind can shine into theirs, since all lamps of God were lit by the same spark.

Examples of Applications for Chapter Ten

1. I no longer weaken myself by creating illnesses to replace God.

2. I awaken to the fact that I am already at home in God right now and that I am perfect in God. I place no other gods before Him (such as the god of sickness).

3. Sickness and death were bad habits that I have had. As I remember my own identity, I realize that these things are unnecessary.

4. I am now completely forgiven for the blasphemous times I denied who I was. I forgive the church for teaching me the wrong definition of blasphemy.

5. I acknowledge that, since God has given me freedom to choose (free will), I am the one totally responsible. Now I accept myself as God created me. I acknowledge Him as my creator.

6. I can help heal others by seeing them as healed. I do not go into agreement with their belief systems and I do not add fear.

7. I see in sick people the love of God and peace. I strengthen that in them. My presence alone, grounded in spirit, will make them strong.

On a separate piece of paper, make a list of your own applications.

D*uring the ten days you are studying Chapter Ten*
in the Text, learn one lesson a day in the workbook,
summarizing what you learned in this space.

Day 91: _____

Day 92: _____

Day 93: _____

Day 94: _____

Day 95: _____

Day 96: _____

Day 97: _____

Day 98: _____

Day 99: _____

Day 100: _____

Chapter Eleven

The Ego and God are diametrically opposed in all respects. The authority problem is always your source of conflict. Are you choosing the ego or God as your authority? Your decision is always an answer to the question "Who is my Father?" Nothing alive is fatherless. Life is creation. The ego is merely a delusional system where you made your own Father. If you believe you are absent from God, you will believe He is absent from you. The projection of the ego makes you believe God's will is not yours. Then it seems God demands of you what you do not want to give and deprives you of what you want.

Jesus comes from the Father to offer you everything again. The Holy Spirit remembers what God's will is for you, since you don't. But *the invitation to the Holy Spirit must come from you.* Whom you invite will abide in you. (The Holy Spirit cannot speak to an unwelcoming host because it will not be heard. Whenever you ask the ego to enter, you lessen Its welcome.) Think like the Holy Spirit as much as possible so it becomes your only Guest. Would you be hostage to the ego or host to God? You are free to determine who should be your Guest and how long He shall remain.

Jesus holds the door open for you. But in order to be worthy to dwell in the temple, you must accept and bless the whole Sonship. The Sonship is yourself. All blame must be undone. As you withdraw blame from others, there is a strong tendency to harbor it within. But self-blame is still ego identification. Only the ego blames. You cannot enter God's presence if you attack His Son. The Sonship is your salvation.

If you knew what God wills for you, your joy would be complete.

you would see such beauty that your joy would not be able to be contained! Out of your joy you would create beauty in His name. (It cannot be told what this is like because you are not ready.) The way is not hard, but it is very different. Your way has been the way of pain, which is very hard indeed. Fear and grief have been your guests. You cannot enter God's presence with those guests. Nor can you enter alone. All your brothers and sisters must enter with you.

Immortality is His will for you. Glory is your inheritance.

Examples of Applications for Chapter Eleven

1. I acknowledge that God is my Father and everpresent for me. He is always available.

2. I was wrong when I thought God would make me sacrifice and would deprive me. God's will for me is perfect happiness, and he wants to give me what I want.

3. I ask my old guests, fear and pain, to leave. I invite the Holy Spirit as my guest and make Him welcome to remain.

4. I withdraw blame from others and I am careful not to blame myself. I remember that all blame is off the track. I know this is not the way to enter the Kingdom.

5. I do not blame my mate. I ask myself what am I getting out of having that situation he or she seems to be making. What is my payoff? I take responsibility for *everything* that happens in my space.

6. I am completely open to the joy, the beauty, and the Immortality God has to offer. I now receive the gifts of the Kingdom.

7. I appreciate Jesus for showing the way.

On a separate piece of paper, make a list of your own applications.

D*uring the ten days you are studying Chapter Eleven*
in the Text, learn one lesson a day in the workbook,
summarizing what you learned in this space.

Day 101: _____

Day 102: _____

Day 103: _____

Day 104: _____

Day 105: _____

Day 106: _____

Day 107: _____

Day 108: _____

Day 109: _____

Day 110: _____

Chapter Twelve

*E*very loving thought is true; everything is an appeal for healing or help (regardless of the form it takes). *Fear is a call for love.* (Fear and love are the only true emotions.) *You are fearful of yourself!*

When you identify with the ego it makes you feel poor and deprived. You then experience depression and anger because you exchanged self-love for self-hate, making you afraid of yourself.

Whenever you become angry with a sister or brother, you are believing that the ego is to be saved by attack. Those who attack are poor. Poverty is of the ego, never of God. In order to get rid of your hatred, you have to believe that it is in your mind and not outside.

Your world has been one of separation. You may even be willing to accept death to deny your Father. Those who see true reality cannot see the world of death. Death is not of the real world. In the real world everything reflects the eternal. But you have nailed yourself to the cross and placed a crown of thorns on your head. Your belief is that power comes from sacrifice and pain.

If you are afraid when you look within, it is because you see something that is not there. The ego fully believes that you are a criminal and deserving of death. *The death penalty is the ego's ultimate goal.* By confusing yourself with the ego, you believe you want death. When you are tempted to yield to the desire for death, *remember that Jesus did not die.* Would eternal life have been given Him and not you? When you learn to make Christ manifest, you will never see death.

The Resurrection represents what you want to be. The Resurrection is the symbol of joy. It is the complete triumph of Christ over the ego by transcendence. You can teach that Jesus did not die by demonstrating that He lives in you.

The ego engages you in an intense search for love, yet it teaches you love is dangerous. Therefore, its motto is "Seek love but do not find it." The ego cannot love. It distorts love. You do not know the meaning of love and that is your handicap. The curriculum you have chosen is against love—all it amounts to is a course in how to attack yourself!

Christ waits for you. Jesus is the manifestation of the Holy Spirit. When you see Him it will be because you have invited Him. The Holy Spirit is invisible, but you can see the results of Its presence. Miracles speak for Its presence. Christ is invisible to you because of what you made visible. When you made visible what is not true, then what is visible becomes invisible to you.

Because of your Father's love you can never forget Him. You can deny it, but you can't lose it.

Offer love and it will come to you because love is drawn to itself.

Examples of Applications for Chapter Twelve

1. When someone is upset or afraid, or a disturbance in my space, I remember they are appealing for help. I always turn up the love and calmly ask, "How can I assist you?"

2. I remember for myself that anger and attack are not of God and never justified. I can accomplish more without anger. If I begin to get angry, I remember that my hatred only comes from within me. I choose to give it up.

3. I forgive myself for wanting to kill life. I forgive myself for "buying into" the idea of death. I forgive myself for projecting that death came from God.

4. I relinquish my investment in death. I let go of the thought that death is inevitable.

5. I can live eternally since I am one with God. I can also dematerialize and rematerialize (i.e., translate and ascend).

6. The end of the world is not destruction but translation. I contribute my part by letting the Holy Spirit teach me, and how to teach this to others.

7. I thank God that Jesus came to teach me translation.

On a separate piece of paper, make a list of your own applications.

During the ten days you are studying Chapter Twelve in the Text, learn one lesson a day in the workbook, summarizing what you learned in this space.

Day 111: Review Chapters 91 and 92 _____

Day 112: Review Chapters 93 and 94 _____

Day 113: Review Chapters 95 and 96 _____

Day 114: Review Chapters 97 and 98_____

Day 115: Review Chapters 99 and 100_____

Day 116: Review Chapters 101 and 102_____

Day 117: Review Chapters 103 and 104_____

Day 118: Review Chapters 105 and 106_____

Day 119: Review Chapters 107 and 108_____

Day 120: Review Chapters 109 and 110_____

WARNING
You May Be Tempted To Not Go On With This Book.

We tend to avoid what we need the most. This course has a goal for your happiness and peace and yet you are afraid of it. To some extent you believe that by not learning it you are protecting yourself. In the extreme, you are afraid of redemption and you think it will kill you.

Do not let the ego tempt you to stop now because of this fear. You have come this far and deserve to be acknowledged.

Chapter Thirteen

God is thought of as cruel because we are born into this world in pain, grow up attended by suffering, and as adults learn sorrow, separation and death. If this were the real world, God *would* be cruel.

To the ego there is no escape from guilt. Guilt hides Christ from your sight. As long as you believe the Son of God is guilty, you will walk the carpet leading to death. The ultimate purpose of projection, you think, is to get rid of guilt, yet you are just concealing it. The ego's destructive urge is so great that nothing short of crucifixion can ultimately satisfy it. The ego does want to kill you. The ego thinks it is God, and *guiltlessness is actually interpreted as the final guilt which fully justifies murder.*

Love and guilt cannot coexist. When you have accepted the Atonement for yourself, you will realize there is no guilt in you.

You are not really afraid of the crucifixion. Your real terror is of *redemption.* Your fear of attack is nothing compared to your fear of love. The memory of God is covered over by your hostility and hatred. *You do not want the separation healed.* You secretly know that, by removing that dark cloud, your love for your Father would impel you to answer his call and leap into Heaven. *You want to hide your intense, burning love for God.* You think God's love would reduce you to ashes, make you little, make you into nothingness. Your individual death seems more valuable than your living Oneness. You are more afraid of God than the ego. Real Heaven is the greatest threat you think you could experience.

You have two true emotions: love and fear. You react to love with fear and draw away from it. Fear attracts you.

The ego cannot tolerate release from the past. You consider it natural to use your past experience as the reference point from which to judge the present. Yet this is unnatural because it is delusional. Stay in the present. Others' errors are all past. By perceiving them without sin, you are releasing them. See no one as guilty.

To attain the real world, you must deny the world you see. You do not want the one you see—it has disappointed you since the beginning of time. Everything the ego tells you that you need will hurt you. Do not ask yourself what you need because you do not know. Only the Holy Spirit knows what you need.

God gave you the Holy Spirit to remove all the doubt and guilt you laid upon yourself. The Holy Spirit will restore your sanity. Lay before His eternal sanity all your hurt and let Him heal you. Do not leave any spot of pain hidden from His light.

Accepting the Atonement teaches you what immortality is. You are immortal because you are eternal.

Examples of Applications for Chapter Thirteen

1. I affirm my own guiltlessness. I am innocent. My innocence is holy. It is right and good to be claiming my guiltlessness. I give up guilt and allow myself to experience the love that is there in its place.

2. I do want the separation healed and I do want to be with my Father. I am willing to feel my burning love for God the Father.

3. With love I call the real world to me.

4. I release the past. I see the reality that others are my brothers and sisters. Their errors are past. I see them without errors.

5. I no longer use my experience to judge the present. Just because I failed at something does not mean I must fail now. Failure is of the ego and not of God.

6. The Holy Spirit leads me to Christ, and where else would I go? I have no other need but to awake in Him. (This world I have made does not give me what I really want.)

7. I lay at the feet of the Holy Spirit all my hurt, pain and fear. I leave nothing hidden. I have nothing to hide.

On a separate piece of paper, make a list of your own applications.

During the ten days you are studying Chapter Thirteen
in the Text, learn one lesson a day in the workbook,
summarizing what you learned in this space.

Day 121: _____

Day 122: _____

Day 123: _____

Day 124: _____

Day 125: _____

Day 126: _____

Day 127: _____

Day 128: _____

Day 129: _____

Day 130: _____

Chapter Fourteen

The ego points to darkness and death, but your thought system has become so twisted that you cannot see it leads to nothing. The logic of the world leads to nothing, for its goal is nothing. Do not underestimate the insanity of the world.

You who are steadfastly devoted to misery must first recognize that you are miserable and not happy. You actually believe misery is happiness. The simple truth is alien to you because simplicity is difficult.

You must become a happy learner. You must realize that everything you've learned is distorted. You must give everything you have learned to the Holy Spirit to be undone for you. Decide now for guiltlessness. The guiltless learner learns easily because his thoughts are free. Each hour, minute and second you are choosing between the ego and the Holy Spirit. The ego is the choice for guilt. The Holy Spirit is the choice for guiltlessness. When the pain of guilt attracts you, remember if you yield to it you are deciding against happiness.

No penalty is ever asked of you—except by yourself. Teach no one he has hurt you—for then you teach yourself that what is not of God has power over you.

Another thing you need to unlearn is isolation. You taught yourself the unnatural habit of not communicating with your Creator. You need to decide that you are wrong about yourself and decide that God is right. When you learn to decide with God, all decisions become as easy as breathing. The Holy Spirit will answer without delay every question about what to do.

Do not ask to be forgiven, for this has already been accomplished. Ask rather to learn how to forgive.

Everything you have taught yourself has made your power more obscure to you. The essential thing for you to learn is that *You do not know.* All your dark lessons must be brought willingly to truth. Bring to Him every secret you have locked away.

Earth can reflect heaven or hell, God or the ego. The Atonement offers you God. (The Atonement, however, does not make you holy. You were created holy. It merely brings unholiness to holiness.) God's graciousness will cover all your sense of pain and loss with the immortal assurance of His love. Fear of death will be replaced by the joy of life.

The power of God is limitless. The number of miracles you can perform is limitless. However, you have no conception of limitless yet. You are bound to form and not to content. The ego is incapable of understanding content. It enjoys studying itself and analyzing, yet it studies form with meaningless content. You must let the Holy Spirit order your thoughts on this.

The test of truth, to see if you have learned God's lesson, is this:

1. Are you wholly free of fear of any kind?
2. Do all those you meet (and even those who think of you) share in your perfect peace?

Don't think you understand anything until you have passed this test of perfect peace!

Examples of Applications for Chapter Fourteen

1. I take the direction pointing to Heaven and aliveness.

2. I forgive myself, and let go of making my mind complex and choosing misery over happiness. I now know the difference.

3. I am willing to unlearn all that I learned that was inappropriate, even if that means everything so far. I ask to be taught. I abandon the teacher of attack and take the teacher of peace.

4. I make no one guilty. When it appears someone has hurt me, I remember I can only hurt myself with the thought that the ego has power over me.

5. I decide God is right and I decide with God. I accept that I am already forgiven.

6. I accept that I do not know.

7. I expose all my sins and areas of darkness. I have nothing to hide.

On a separate piece of paper, make a list of your own applications.

During the ten days you are studying Chapter Fourteen
in the Text, learn one lesson a day in the workbook,
summarizing what you learned in this space.

Day 131: _____

Day 132: _____

Day 133: _____

Day 134: _____

Day 135: _____

Day 136: _____

Day 137: _____

Day 138: _____

Day 139: _____

Day 140: _____

Chapter Fifteen

To the ego the goal is death, and it uses time to convince you of the inevitability of death. It craves death for you, but even that leaves it unsatisfied. It likes to convince you that it can pursue you after the grave. Therefore you cannot find peace even in death. It offers you immortality in hell. Hell is its goal. The belief in hell is inescapable to those who identify with the ego.

The Holy Spirit teaches you there is no hell. Hell is only what the ego made of the present. Take this instant and think of it as all there is. Could you not give an instant to the Holy Spirit and let yourself have immortality and joy now? The Holy Instant is this instant and every instant. It is a time when you receive and give perfect communication. This means your mind is open both to receive and give. It is the recognition that all minds are in communion. It accepts everything.

The *Course* tells you to *be not content with littleness*. Littleness is the offering you give yourself. It is your evaluation of yourself. But you will not have peace if you choose littleness. Littleness is of the ego. You will be content only with magnitude, which is your home. You do not even have to strive for it. You already have it. Jesus calls to you to make the Holy Instant yours at once for the release of littleness.

To limit love to only part of the Sonship is to bring guilt into your relationships (because separation is the source of guilt). You cannot love part of reality and understand what love means. If you would love what is unlike to God, who knows no special love, how can you understand it? If you believe special love relationships can offer you salvation, then you believe separation is salvation. All special relationships have elements of fear in them because of the guilt. That is why they shift and change so frequently. Love cannot be depended upon where fear has entered.

The Holy Spirit knows no one is special. But He also knows you have made special relationships. He won't let you destroy them if you will only let Him purify them. He can translate them into holiness. Place your relationships under His care.

It is impossible to condemn part of a relationship and find peace in it. All relationships are seen as total commitments, and one does not need to conflict with another.

The ego establishes relationships only to get something. Each one thinks he has sacrificed something to the other and hates him for it. These relationships are forged out of anger, and the ego counsels you that the more anger you invest outside yourself, the softer you become. In these angry alliances each seeks relief from guilt by increasing it in the other, believing that this decreases guilt in him. These relationships are dedicated to continuation of loneliness. The ego teaches you that loneliness is solved by guilt. This is clearly insane.

To the ego, a relationship means that bodies are together. The body is content as long as it is there to receive its sacrifice. The ego limits your perception of others to the body.

The special love relationship is the big distraction you use to obscure your attention to God the Father. You think special relationships save you from God, whose total love you think would destroy you! The only relationship that has meaning is God's relationship with you. *There is no other love that can satisfy you.* Being complete, it asks for nothing. Everyone joined in it has everything. Relate only with what will never leave you, and what you cannot leave.

Your confusion of sacrifice and love is so profound that you cannot conceive of love without sacrifice. To you, total love would be total sacrifice. That is why you are so terrified of God. If God demands total sacrifice, you think you would be better to project Him away from you. You think the ego demands less of you.

This is a time of rebirth! Give the Holy Spirit everything that would hurt you. Let your relationships be made Holy.

Examples of Applications for Chapter Fifteen

1. I forgive myself for believing in hell and death. I relinquish these notions now and forever.

2. In each Holy Instant, I make a clean, untarnished birth.

3. I trade in my littleness and I accept my magnitude. I give up all limiting thoughts (such as "I can't" or "I am not good enough"). I release all littleness.

4. I strive to love all people equally rather than making one or a few special. I do not make my relationships about sacrifice or guilt. I do not try to make my mate guilty.

5. I no longer use special relationships to keep me from God. My mate is not special. My relationship is not special. I do not make anyone more special than God, than others, or than myself.

6. I turn over my relationship to the Holy Spirit for purification. My commitment is total to all my relationships, and one does not interfere with the others because I do not let it.

7. I say to my sister or brother: "I give you to the Holy Spirit as part of myself. I know that you will be released, unless I want to use you to imprison myself. In the name of my freedom I choose your release, because I recognize that we will be released together."

On a separate piece of paper, make a list of your own applications.

*During the ten days you are studying Chapter Fifteen
in the Text, learn one lesson a day in the workbook,
summarizing what you learned in this space.*

Day 141: Review Chapters 121 and 122_____

Day 142: Review Chapters 123 and 124_____

Day 143: Review Chapters 125 and 126_____

Day 144: Review Chapters 127 and 128_____

Day 145: Review Chapters 129 and 130_____

Day 146: Review Chapters 131 and 132_____

Day 147: Review Chapters 133 and 134_____

Day 148: Review Chapters 135 and 136_____

Day 149: Review Chapters 137 and 138_____

Day 150: Review Chapters 139 and 140_____

Chapter Sixteen

Most of this chapter is about the tyranny of special relationships and exposing what the *Course* calls "the special hate relationship." (The hatred here is merely more apparent and the relationship is clearly one of anger and attack. Someone becomes the focus of anger and we cherish everything he has done to hurt us.) Don't be afraid to look at it—your freedom lies in looking at it.

The special relationship denies our need for God by substituting the need for special people and special things in its place. It rests on the assumption that there is something lacking in us, a special need we think we have. It is founded on our egocentric perception of the other person's capacity to give us what we believe is lacking in ourselves. This is only an illusion of love and nothing more than a veil of hate, since it is based on hatred of ourselves.

It has nothing in common with real love and is always based on exclusion. It entails the belief that love cannot be shared. Hope of salvation is based on one special person, and attention he or she may devote elsewhere is considered a threat. The special relationship is the ego's chosen home. It is the ego's chief weapon for keeping you from heaven.

In looking at the special relationship, realize that it involves a great amount of pain. Anxiety, despair, guilt and attack all enter into it. Hatred is welcome and held together by the illusion of love. If the illusion goes, it is broken and unsatisfying on the grounds of disillusionment. Where disillusionment is possible, there was not love but hate. Each partner tries to sacrifice the self he does not want for one he thinks he would prefer, and then feels guilty for the sin of taking while giving nothing of value in return. When both see this special self in each other, the ego sees a "union made in Heaven." Neither recognizes he has asked for hell.

Love is seen as an escape from death, yet when partners find the fear of death still upon them, the love relationship loses the illusion that it is what it is not. Fear rushes in. The special relationship is an attempt to bring love into fear.

The conviction of littleness lies in every special relationship, for only the deprived can value specialness. *When two individuals seek to become one, they are trying to decrease their magnitude,* for God is left out. The central theme is that God must die young so you can live. It is all acted out through your own death. (An altar is erected between two people on which each seeks to kiss his or her self, and on the body raise another self that takes its power from death. This ritual is repeated over and over.)

The special relationship is a ritual of *form* to take the place of God at the expense of *content*. The search for the special relationship is the sign that you equate yourself with the ego and not with God. Since it fosters guilt, it imprisons. Love is freedom.

The special relationship takes vengeance on the past. It holds the past against you. It is impossible to let go of the past without relinquishing the special relationship.

You will go through this undoing quite unharmed and at last emerge as yourself. This is the last step in readiness for God. Across the bridge it is so different, but in transition there may be some confusion and disorientation. Whenever you are attracted to the special relationship, enter with Him into the Holy Instant and there He will release you. The Holy Spirit knows that completion lies first in union with God and then in extension of that union.

Be wholly willing to abandon all illusions. In any relationship in which you are wholly willing to accept completion (and only this) there is God completed, and His Son with Him.

To join in close relationship with Him is to accept relationships as real and, through their reality, to give up all illusions for the reality of your relationship with God. Forgive us our illusions, Father.

Examples of Applications for Chapter Sixteen

1. I am willing to expose all my relationships. I bring them to sight, and do not try to hide even the hate.

2. I no longer use special relationships to deny my need for God.

3. There is nothing lacking in me. I do not need a special person to complete me.

4. I do not limit my love to just one special person, nor expect him to stop loving others because of me.

5. I let go of the past and the illusion and insanity of the special relationship.

6. I pray to be forgiven now for putting other gods before Him and decreasing my magnitude.

7. I am a whole individual. I attract another whole individual. I love myself, therefore I don't need another self to replace me.

8. I no longer make form more important than love. I remember that love is always more important than form.

9. I turn over my relationship to the Holy Spirit to be used for His purpose, and enter with Him into the Holy Instant.

On a separate piece of paper, make a list of your own applications.

During the ten days you are studying Chapter Sixteen
in the Text, learn one lesson a day in the workbook,
summarizing what you learned in this space.

Day 151: _____

Day 152: _____

Day 153: _____

Day 154: _____

Day 155: _____

Day 156: _____

Day 157: _____

Day 158: _____

Day 159: _____

Day 160: _____

Chapter Seventeen

You must bring your fantasies to truth. The bridge to the forgiven world is easy to cross. The real world is attained simply by the complete forgiveness of the old. To forgive is merely to remember only the loving thoughts you gave in the past, and those that were given to you. All the rest must be forgotten. *Forgiveness is selective remembering.*

The unholy relationships you have with shadow figures from the past have as their purpose the exclusion of truth. Whatever reminds you of your past grievances attracts you. These relationships are attempts at union through the body, for only bodies can be seen as a means of vengeance. In an unholy relationship it is not even the body of the other with which union is attempted, but the bodies of those who are not there, so the attempt at union becomes a way of excluding even the one with whom the union was sought!

Every special relationship you have made is a substitute for God's will and glorifies your own instead. Every special relationship has as its purpose the aim of occupying your mind so completely that you will not hear the call for Truth.

Jesus has said repeatedly that the Holy Spirit would not deprive you of your special relationships, but would transform them. He restores to them the function given them by God. Offer your relationship to the Holy Spirit for its purpose. The holy relationship is the old unholy relationship transformed and seen anew. It is the complete reversal of the unholy relationship.

The only difficult phase is in the beginning when the goal of the relationship is abruptly shifted to the exact opposite of what it was.

93

Although disturbed and distressing, *the temptation of the ego becomes extremely intense with this shift.* The ego may tell you to substitute this relationship for yet another one and return to your former goals. Getting rid of your partner may seem like the solution. *This is the time for faith.*

There is no problem in any situation that faith will not solve. If you lack faith, ask that it be restored. Your faith must grow to meet the new goal. Holiness and faith go hand in hand.

God established His relationship with you to make you happy; thus forever the function of relationships became to make us happy and nothing else.

Examples of Applications for Chapter Seventeen

1. I completely forgive the old world. I remember only the love and choose to forget the rest.

2. I no longer set up my mate to be someone in my past. He or she is not my mother, not my father, not my ex, not anyone with whom I was formerly incomplete.

3. I no longer use a special relationship to distract myself from the Heavenly Father.

4. I allow the goal to be shifted in my relationship. During the time this causes uneasiness, I call for help in strengthening my faith. I pray that my faith be restored.

5. I always remember that the purpose of my relationship is to share the light and to make happiness.

6. I ask myself what I want to come of this relationship. I see that I want the goal of truth and the result of peace.

On a separate piece of paper, make a list of your own applications.

*During the ten days you are studying Chapter Seventeen
in the Text, learn one lesson a day in the workbook,
summarizing what you learned in this space.*

Day 161: _____

Day 162: _____

Day 163: _____

Day 164: _____

Day 165: _____

Day 166: _____

Day 167: _____

Day 168: _____

Day 169: _____

Day 170: _____

Chapter Eighteen

You substituted fragmentation for wholeness, illusion for truth, and fear for God. The magnitude of this error is so vast and incredible that from it a whole world of unreality emerged. Dreams (waking or sleeping) are all chaotic because they are governed by conflicting wishes. Dreams are perceptual temper tantrums. In dreams you arrange everything and reality is outrageously violated. *All your time is spent in dreaming. Your sleeping and waking dreams have different forms. That is all.* In your waking dreams, the special relationship is the way you hold onto unreality. Your goal in all of these dreams is darkness.

Do you believe He would leave you in darkness if you agreed to leave it to God? Now that you have called upon truth, it is rushing to meet you. You are made whole in your desire to make whole. The first change is that dreams of fear are changed to happy dreams, your special relationship is changed from pain and guilt to a source of joy, and freedom and your unholiness is changed to holiness.

Because you believe you can get and give something else besides perfect oneness, guilt has entered and you hate your mind. You have displaced your hate and guilt to your body, which suffers and dies because it is attacked by you. By using your body as a scapegoat for guilt, you are making it an enemy, weak, vulnerable and treacherous. God cannot enter an abode that harbors vengeance, violence and death. *You have locked yourself in a separate prison. You hate it and would destroy it.*

You need utterly to forget about the body. You are not your body. (You still have too much faith in it as a source of strength. You constantly make plans for its comfort and protection.) The body is merely a small sunbeam to the sun, a ripple on the surface of the ocean. In its arrogance it has decided it is the sun! Forget about the body and make a place in you where it ceases to demand attention. It only takes an instant for the Atonement to happen. Afterwards you will see the body again, but not quite the same.

The Holy Instant is the result of your determination to be holy. It is the *Answer*. The desire and willingness to let it come precedes its coming. The way you prepare for it is by recognizing that you want it above all else. God can take you to what lies underneath insanity if you are willing to follow the Holy Spirit through seeming terror. Do not be stopped by dark clouds of fear. The Holy Instant is your invitation for love to enter into your bleak kingdom and transform it.

There is nothing outside you. Heaven is not a place or a condition. Heaven is merely an awareness, a perfect oneness and the knowledge that there is nothing else. It is a world of shining light and innocence. The step beyond forgiveness will be taken by God, when you will be transported to something completely different.

Examples of Applications for Chapter Eighteen

1. I pray to be awakened from the chaotic dreams that I have made. My goal is to come out of darkness into the light.

2. I trade in fearful dreams for happy dreams. I trade in the pain and guilt of my relationships for joy and freedom in them. I trade in all my unholiness for holiness.

3. I remember my oneness and let go of all guilt, so I no longer use my body to punish myself. My body is innocent. I forgive myself for misusing the body.

4. My body is not for attack, nor does it need my constant attention and protection because I am not my body. I am a Light Being with all the safety of God, since I am one with God.

5. I allow my body to be transformed in the Holy Instant. I desire the Holy Instant above all else.

6. Prayer: "I who am host to God am worthy of Him. There is no need to make it ready for Him, only that I do not interfere with His plan; I need add nothing to His plan, but to receive it I must be willing not to substitute my own in place of it. I am willing."

7. I forgive everyone who taught me heaven was somewhere else and I forgive myself for believing it. I can have heaven right now by remembering perfect oneness and knowledge and that that is all there is.

On a separate piece of paper, make a list of your own applications.

During the ten days you are studying Chapter Eighteen
in the Text, learn one lesson a day in the workbook,
summarizing what you learned in this space.

Day 171: Review Lessons 151 and 152 _____

Day 172: Review Lessons 153 and 154 _____

Day 173: Review Lessons 155 and 156 _____

Day 174: Review Lessons 157 and 158_____

Day 175: Review Lessons 159 and 160_____

Day 176: Review Lessons 161 and 162_____

Day 177: Review Lessons 163 and 164_____

Day 178: Review Lessons 165 and 166_____

Day 179: Review Lessons 167 and 168_____

Day 180: Review Lessons 169 and 170_____

Chapter Nineteen

When a situation is dedicated wholly to truth, peace is inevitable. But peace without faith will never be attained.

First it is essential that you do not confuse error with sin. Sin is something the ego made up. Sin is the idea of evil that cannot be corrected. (If sin were really possible, it would be irreversible.) Sin calls for punishment. To the ego, the acceptance of the self as sinful is perceived as holiness. To the ego, purity is seen as arrogance. Sin is the proclamation that attack is real and guilt is justified. If sin is real, both you and God are not.

The child of God can be mistaken, he can deceive himself, he can even turn the power of his mind against himself, but he cannot sin. Error can be corrected and made right. (Punishment, however, is not correction.) The Holy Spirit cannot punish sin, for It knows not sin. The Holy Spirit recognizes mistakes and would correct them all.

If you believe in sin you will believe in death. To the ego sin means death, and so the Atonement is achieved through murder! You will be healed of this idea of sin the instant you give it no power.

The Obstacles to Peace

Obstacle 1: The Desire to Get Rid of It

You still have a little insane wish to get rid of Him even though you invited Him. You are still attracted to guilt and you cherish evil and sin. All of this produces fear of love. You still cherish remnants of attack and so you still desire to get rid of peace. But this is just a feather compared to the wings of truth.

Obstacle 2: The Belief That the Body is Valuable for What It Offers

The body has no purpose of itself, only what is given it. The body can bring you neither peace nor turmoil, pain nor pleasure. The mind rules the body. The body is a means, not an end. Equating your self with the body is an invitation to pain. The ego tells the body to search for pain. (You are attracted to pain.) The body gets the idea that pain is pleasure!

The Holy Spirit does not demand you sacrifice the home of the body's pleasure. Pain is the only sacrifice it asks and this He would remove.

Obstacle 3: The Attraction of Death

No one can die unless he chooses death. Death is a result of the thought we call the ego (as surely as life is the result of the thought called God). If death were true, it would be the complete disruption of communication, which is the ego's goal. You are attracted to death and dedicated to it. Look at those who fear death and see how loudly and often they call to it. You are the one who commands your body to die.

Ask not for release of the body, but free it from the merciless orders you yourself laid upon it.

Obstacle 4: The Fear of God

What you would see without the fear of death is the remembrance of your Father. If fear of death were gone, what could you fear but life? *You are not afraid of death or the ego. These are your chosen "friends." You made a deal with them, agreeing never to have the veil (fear of God) lifted.*

Fear of God is the final step in your disassociation. You are afraid of God because you think He kills people and because you fear your sisters and brothers. Those you do not forgive, you fear. Think who your brother is before you condemn him. Offer thanks that he is holy. Heaven is the gift you owe your sister. Offer her forgiveness and give her joy. The redeemed give joy because they have been healed of pain.

In the quiet recognition that you love God, the desire to get rid of peace fades.

Examples of Applications for Chapter Nineteen

1. I now allow the Holy Spirit to undo all my confusion about sin and error. There is no sin and my errors can be corrected.

2. I forgive myself for thinking that being sinful made me holy; and I forgive those who taught me this in church.

3. Now I can let go of the concept of punishment. I merely allow my errors to be corrected by the Holy Spirit.

4. I choose peace. I am careful to notice my temptation to create arguments, fights and war out of habit, in order to get rid of peace.

5. I am not my body. My brother is not his body. I am no longer attracted to pain. I forgive myself for thinking pain is pleasure.

6. I am now clear that death is a result of a thought and therefore all death is suicide. No one outside of me can kill me unless I make that happen. Now I give my body new orders: Since I was the thinker that thought death is inevitable, I am also the thinker that can think *life is inevitable* and I am safe and immortal.

7. I give up my fear of God and fear of life. I want communion, I want salvation, I want my Father.

8. When anything seems to cause me fear, I pray this: Teach me how not to make of this an obstacle to peace. I let you use it for me.

On a separate piece of paper, make a list of your own applications.

During the ten days you are studying Chapter Nineteen
in the Text, learn one lesson a day in the workbook,
summarizing what you learned in this space.

Day 181: _____

Day 182: _____

Day 183: _____

Day 184: _____

Day 185: _____

Day 186: _____

Day 187: _____

Day 188: _____

Day 189: _____

Day 190: _____

Chapter Twenty

Do you like what you have made? A world of murder and attack, where you thread your way through constant dangers, alone and frightened—hoping at best that death will wait a little longer? *You made this up!* It is a picture of what you think you are and how you see yourself. This sickly picture of yourself is carefully preserved by the ego. How happy has this puff of madness made you?

What if you recognized this world as a hallucination? What if you really understood you made it up with your ego mind? Hallucinations disappear when they are recognized for what they are. All you need to do is recognize that *you did this!* But prisoners bound with heavy chains for years do not leap up in joy the instant they are made free. It takes awhile to understand what freedom is.

Remember, nothing can hurt you unless you give it the power to do so. *You* gave power to sin, misery, sickness, pain and death.

The body is the ego's chosen weapon for seeking power through relationships. This is but an idolatry. An unholy relationship is no relationship. It is a state of isolation. Offer another thorns and you are crucified. He who offers thorns to anyone is acting against the Christ.

See others as sinless and there can be no fear in you. Offer them the gift of lilies, the gift of love. Look with different eyes upon them. It is impossible to overestimate their value. God's Son comes closest to himself in a holy relationship.

The Holy Relationship reflects the true relationship the Son of God has with His Father. The Holy Spirit rests within it, in the certainty it will endure forever. In your brother or sister is the light of God's eternal promise of your immortality. Enter together into paradise and know the peace of God. Walk together into God's everlasting arms. You will call the hearts of everyone, and in your gift of two voices raised together is everyone made glad.

Vision will come to you at first in glimpses, but that will be enough. Peace will come to all who ask for it with real desire and sincerity. Easter is a sign of peace, not pain. A slain Christ has no meaning, but a risen Christ becomes the symbol of the Son of God's forgiveness of himself.

Now we celebrate life!

Examples of Applications for Chapter Twenty

1. I confess that I made up pain, misery and death and this has not made me happy; but I *am* responsible. I did this.

2. I am willing to learn what freedom is.

3. I cannot be hurt unless I give something power to hurt me. Therefore all blame is off the track.

4. I see my brother as sinless. I am committed to see him differently than I have. I constantly appreciate the value he provides for me to see myself.

5. I pray that all my relationships become holy and immortal.

6. My partner and I dedicate our relationship to the Holy Spirit and share the light with the world. I allow the Holy Spirit to teach us the means.

7. I celebrate life and the Resurrection.

On a separate piece of paper, make a list of your own applications.

*During the ten days you are studying Chapter Twenty
in the Text, learn one lesson a day in the workbook,
summarizing what you learned in this space.*

Day 191: _____

Day 192: _____

Day 193: _____

Day 194: _____

Day 195: _____

Day 196: _____

Day 197: _____

Day 198: _____

Day 199: _____

Day 200: _____

Chapter Twenty-One

The world you see is what you gave it, nothing more. As a man thinketh, so does he perceive. *Seek not to change the world, but choose to change your mind about the world.* What you need for true vision is to say "I am responsible for what I see." You are deceiving yourself when you think you are helpless. What happens to you is your choice. If you are suffering, sin was your goal.

The Holy Spirit will never teach you that you are sinful. The ego, however, tells you never to look within or you will see sin and God will strike you blind. The ego's vision looks within and sees you as tiny, vulnerable and afraid. You therefore experience depression, worthlessness, unreality and feelings of impermanence.

The other vision in which your freedom lies sees miracles as natural as breathing. But you must replace madness with reason.

Madness sees sin.

> Reason cannot see sin; it sees only errors and their correction.

Madness says you must be separate since you have a body.

> Reason says the body does not separate me from my brother. Reason says you are joined, how could you have private thoughts?

Madness is an attack on reason.

> Reason does not attack, but takes the place of madness.

Madness is going for misery and helplessness.

Reason says heaven is what you want.

Are you willing to exchange the world of sin for what the Holy Spirit sees? If the answer is sincerely yes, then happiness and constant joy are yours. All that is asked is that you make room for truth. All you are asked to do is *let it in.*

Faith and belief and vision are the means by which the goal of holiness is reached. Through them the Holy Spirit leads you to the real world.

Examples of Applications for Chapter Twenty-One

1. I replace madness with reason. The truth is obvious.

2. I am now going to see errors only—not sin. I will remember that I am joined and not separate, and that is my salvation. Finally, I acknowledge that Heaven is what I want and I can have it here and now.

3. This means that I do not make real all the pain, misery, terror and death I see around me.

4. I make room for the truth, which is the real world.

5. I am not helpless. Everything that happens to me is my choice. There are no accidents.

On a separate piece of paper, make a list of your own applications.

During *the ten days you are studying Chapter Twenty-One*
in the Text, learn one lesson a day in the workbook,
summarizing what you learned in this space.

Day 201: Review Lesson 181 _____

Day 202: Review Lesson 182 _____

Day 203: Review Lesson 183 _____

Day 204: Review Lesson 184_____

Day 205: Review Lesson 185_____

Day 206: Review Lesson 186_____

Day 207: Review Lesson 187_____

Day 208: Review Lesson 188_____

Day 209: Review Lesson 189_____

Day 210: Review Lesson 190_____

NOTE

THIS COURSE WILL BE BELIEVED ENTIRELY OR NOT AT ALL, FOR IT IS WHOLLY TRUE OR WHOLLY FALSE, AND CANNOT BE PARTIALLY BELIEVED. You will either escape from misery entirely or not at all. There is no middle ground.

You are now at the branching of the road. When you come to the place where the branch in the road is quite apparent, you cannot go ahead. You must either go one way or another. The whole purpose of coming this far is to decide which branch you will take now.

Chapter Twenty=Two

Any unholy relationship is based on differences where each one thinks the other has what he has not. They come together, each to complete himself and rob the other. They stay until they think there is nothing left to steal, and then move on. And so they wander through a world of strangers, unlike themselves, living with their bodies, perhaps under a common roof that shelters neither—in the same room and yet a world apart.

In an unholy relationship each one is valued because he seems to justify the other's sin. Each sees within the other what impels him to sin against his will. Thus he lays his sins upon the other and is attracted to him to perpetuate his sins.

A holy relationship starts from a different premise. Each one has looked within and seen no lack. Accepting completion, she or he would extend it by joining with another, also whole. Seeing no differences between the selves, each finds there nothing to take. This relationship has heaven's holiness. In each holy relationship is reborn the ability to communicate (instead of separate).

Let not your awareness of others be blocked by your perception of their bodies! Look beyond the bodies upon the Savior that has been given you. A holy relationship must value holiness above all else.

The holy relationship is chosen by God for His own plan. Be thankful that it doesn't serve you. This holy relationship has the power to heal all pain, regardless of its form. Healing lies only in your joint will. In a holy relationship there is no sin.

The service you give the Holy Spirit is service to yourself. You will see your value through your partner's eyes and each is released to see a savior in place of the attacker thought to be there.

To establish a holy relationship requires a unified goal. When two people see their common goal as a search for love in God, a healing takes place. Giving in that relationship then becomes total. There are no wants or needs, only giving, and in that giving both are blessed. That blessing grows and flows to others. The light goes outward to all the world. Seemingly difficult situations are recognized as blessings. There is an opportunity to see Christ in the other without your little ideas of what should be changed or discarded.

In the holy relationship, what one thinks, the other will experience also. What can this mean, except your minds are one? Your relationship is a reflection of the union of the Creator to His Son.

Examples of Applications for Chapter Twenty-Two

1. I no longer need a relationship where "opposites attract," in which someone is developed in areas that I think I am not. I do not need someone else to feel complete. I am complete.

2. I no longer want or need someone else to blame. I am totally responsible. My partner does not make me do anything or become anything. He is not to blame for my behavior.

3. I accept my completion with total self-esteem. I do not need someone else to make me happy. I am happy by myself. I now attract someone else who is complete, who is happy already, with his own self-worth already established.

4. Our communication is natural and telepathic because there is no separation between us. We look beyond our bodies to the fact that we are really light beings and we center our relationship on Christ.

5. Our relationship is dedicated to the plan of the Holy Spirit, not our own.

6. In our relationship, the love is more important than the form.

7. I see my partner as my guru, my mirror, reflecting me so that I constantly see myself. Thus my partner is my Savior.

8. My partner and I have a unified goal. We have dedicated our relationship to something greater than both of us and that is the most important thing.

9. We have a common state of mind, a union where peace is our goal and love is constantly recognized.

10. We have a union where abundance of joy is expressed and all is given to all.

On a separate piece of paper, make a list of your own applications.

*During the ten days you are studying Chapter Twenty-Two
in the Text, learn one lesson a day in the workbook,
summarizing what you learned in this space.*

Day 211: Review Lesson 191 _____

Day 212: Review Lesson 192 _____

Day 213: Review Lesson 193 _____

Day 214: Review Lesson 194_____

Day 215: Review Lesson 195_____

Day 216: Review Lesson 196_____

Day 217: Review Lesson 197_____

Day 218: Review Lesson 198_____

Day 219: Review Lesson 199_____

Day 220: Review Lesson 200_____

NOTE

You have a haunting fear of lack of meaning. It is as though you wandered in without a plan and may just wander off. Denying what you are, you have made up something else. But you do not understand it.

God has no secrets, and He does not lead you through a world of misery, waiting to tell you at journey's end why he did this to you. This *Course* is open to your understanding, and can be understood. That you do not understand it yet is only because your communication is still babyish.

Indeed, your holy relationship is like a baby now in its rebirth.

Chapter Twenty-Three

The ego is at war with God. Do you not realize that a war against yourself is a war against God?

No one can attack unless he thinks he has an enemy. And no one is strong who has an enemy. *What is weak is not the will of God!* War is impossible unless belief in victory is cherished. Conflict within you implies you believe the ego has the power to be victorious. The ego thinks that triumph over you is possible.

The Son of God at war with His Creator is as ridiculous as Nature angry at the wind.

You must be willing to look at the laws you have made that rule the world. There are *laws of chaos*:

1. *That the truth is different for everyone.*
   This maintains that each is separate with a different set of thoughts that set him off from others.

2. *That each one must sin and therefore deserves attack and death.*
   This is the demand that errors call for punishment, not correction. What man has done is interpreted as irrevocable.

3. *That God must accept his Son for what he is and hates him for it.*
   This re-enforces fear of God. If God hates you, it is impossible to turn to Him for help. Salvation is therefore impossible. There is no release and no escape in this system. Only destruction can be the final outcome if you believe this.

4. *The belief that you have what you have taken. Another's loss becomes your gain.*

      This leads to justifying the position of attack to "gain" what has been "withheld."

5. *That there is a substitute for Love.*

      The result: Madness is sanity, illusions are true, attack is kindness, hatred is love, and murder is benediction. This is clearly insane!

If you take a step into this hell you won't recognize the rest.

How can you know whether you chose the stairs to heaven or to hell? Quite easily. *How do you feel?*

Those with the strength of God in their awareness could never think of battle. Everything is given to those who remember Him. But the memory of God comes to the quiet mind. God cannot come where there is conflict.

Open the door of His most holy home. Peace is the state where love abides. God is the only place of safety.

Examples of Applications for Chapter Twenty-Three

1. I confess I have made conflict, provoked arguments and supported battles and war.

2. I confess my biggest mistake was being at war with my Creator.

3. I acknowledge now that sin is not real and therefore punishment and death are not in order.

4. God does not hate me or my sisters and brothers. Salvation is possible.

5. The truth is the same for all and nothing is withheld from me or anyone.

6. Love is the only sanity.

7. Murder is not God's will nor mine. I do not support it.

8. The way I feel always tells me if I am going in the right direction. If I am feeling great, I am going in the right direction.

9. I am one with God and I am innocent. This is my strength.

On a separate piece of paper, make a list of your own applications.

*During the ten days you are studying Chapter Twenty-Three
in the Text, learn one lesson a day in the workbook,
summarizing what you learned in this space.*

Day 221: _____

Day 222: _____

Day 223: _____

Day 224: _____

Day 225: _____

Day 226: _____

Day 227: _____

Day 228: _____

Day 229: _____

Day 230: _____

NOTE

Don't forget that the motivation for this *Course* is the attainment and the keeping of the state of peace.

To learn this *Course* requires willingness to question everything that you hold.

Chapter Twenty-Four

"Specialness" not only sets apart, but also serves to excuse attack on others not "special" as natural and just. Only the "special" could have enemies, for they are "different," and differences of any kind imply orders of reality and the need to judge. What is different calls for judgment, which must come from someone "better."

Specialness is the dictator of wrong decisions—for specialness, it seems, must be defended. The one who is "worse" than you must be attacked so that your specialness can live on his defeat. Specialness is established by a lack seen in another and maintained by searching for lacks. (Comparison is an ego device, as love makes no comparisons.)

The pursuit of specialness is always at the cost of peace. Never can there be peace among the different. *The pursuit of specialness will always bring you pain.* It is the idea of sin made real. You are not special!

Specialness is a lack of trust in anyone but you. Faith is invested in yourself alone. Everything else becomes your enemy and worthy only of destruction. The body demands a special place where God cannot enter. Loneliness is your special kingdom. Your purpose of the body has been specialness. The goal of separation is its curse.

Whatever form of specialness you cherish you have made sin.

Who could hate someone, whose self is his own and whom he knows? Ask yourself these questions and answer truthfully.

1. Would it be possible for you to hate your brother if you were like him?

2. Could you attack him if you realized you journey with him toward the same goal?

3. Wouldn't you help him reach it in every way you could, if his attainment of it were perceived as yours?

You are his enemy in specialness, his friend in shared purpose. Your brother is your friend because his Father created him like you. There is no difference.

NOTE

You would oppose this course because it teaches you are alike.

You are asleep and you hate the call that would awaken you.

You must face this.

NOTE

Don't forget that the healing of God's Son (you) is all the world is for.

If you use it for purposes other than this, you will not escape its laws of violence and death.

You are alike to God as God is to Himself. He is not "special," for He would not keep one part of what He is to Himself. *IT IS THIS YOU FEAR.* For if He is not special, then He willed His Son to be like Him, and your brother is like you. Not special, but possessed of everything, like you.

Forgiveness is the end of specialness. It is the release from all illusion.

See in your sister God's Creation. For in her the Father waits for your acknowledgement that He created you as part of Him. Without you there would be a lack in God. See in your brother's freedom yours, for it is. He is a mirror of yourself. Christ's hand holds *all* his brothers and sisters in Himself. He sings to them of heaven, that their ears may hear no more sounds of battle and of death.

The death of specialness is not your death, but your awakening to life eternal.

Examples of Applications for Chapter Twenty-Four

1. I lay down my judgments and my tendency to make comparisons.

2. I confess that I have tried to be special and I ask for forgiveness.

3. I remember that my father created my sister and brother like me and there is no difference.

4. I am like my sister, therefore I like her. We have the same journey to the same goal. I help her reach it in every way I can. We are friends in our shared purpose.

5. I see my brothers as God's creations. They are like God. I am like God.

6. The sight of Christ is all there is to see, the song of Christ is all there is to hear. The hand of Christ is all there is to hold.

7. All the world is for my healing and others' healing. I do not use it for other purposes.

On a separate piece of paper, make a list of your own applications.

During the ten days you are studying Chapter Twenty-Four
in the Text, learn one lesson a day in the workbook,
summarizing what you learned in this space.

Day 231: _____

Day 232: _____

Day 233: _____

Day 234: _____

Day 235: _____

Day 236: _____

Day 237: _____

Day 238: _____

Day 239: _____

Day 240: _____

Chapter Twenty-Five

Since you believe that you are separate, heaven presents itself to you as separate. But you are *not* separate. What is the same, cannot be different. What is one, cannot have separate parts.

It is extremely hard for those who still believe sin meaningful to understand the Holy Spirit's justice. (They do believe that heaven is hell and *are* afraid of love. They actually believe God's knowledge of justice would be more destructive than the vengeance they love!) Sinners see justice only as their punishment. The laws of sin demand a victim. Death is the cost and must be paid. (This is not justice, but insanity.)

Love is not understandable to sinners because they think justice is split off from love. How can specialness be just? Without impartiality there is no justice. The world, however, solves problems seeing resolution as a state in which it is decided who shall win and who shall lose; how much the one shall attack and how much the other can defend. But the problem remains unsolved.

Isn't it evident that what the body's eyes perceive fills you with fear? Despite your hopes and fancies, despair always results. You see what you believe is there, and you believe it there because you want it there. To the extent that you value guilt, you will perceive a world in which attack is justified. So long as you think that suffering and sin will bring you joy, you will have them.

In everyone you see the reflection of what you wish them to be. The role you give others is given you because it is your judgment on yourself. The state of sinlessness is merely this: The desire to attack is gone. The need for guilt is gone because it has no value. God's justice is impartial. Attack and condemnation are meaningless.

Salvation is God's justice.

Forgiveness is for all. True justice looks on all in the same way. Justice demands no sacrifice. To be just is to be fair and not vengeful. Only justice can set up a state in which there is no loser.

Are you willing to be released from all effects of sin? The Holy Spirit needs this from you: That you prefer It take away what would hurt you to keeping it for yourself. All that is needed is your willingness to forego all values of this world.

"To give a problem to the Holy Spirit to solve for you means that you want it solved. To keep it for yourself to solve without His help, is to decide it should remain unsettled." The Holy Spirit's problem-solving is the way in which the problem ends. It has been solved because it was met with justice. No one deserves to lose.

The Holy Spirit has the power to change the whole foundation of the world you see to one in which nothing is contradicted. It would be madness to entrust salvation to the insane. What is dependable except God's love? Salvation is the *rebirth* of the idea that no one can lose if anyone is to gain. *Justice looks on all the same.*

You have the right to the whole universe, to perfect peace, to complete deliverance from all effects of sin, to life eternal, joyous and complete in every way, as God appointed. Your sister and brother have equal right to miracles.

What is God's belongs to everyone and is our due.

Examples of Applications for Chapter Twenty-Five

1. I do not value sin and guilt.

2. I enter a state of sinlessness and my desire to attack is gone. The need for guilt is gone. It has no purpose.

3. The way I see another is a reflection of what I choose to have him be. The role I give to him is given me. He becomes my judgment of myself.

4. I always set up a win-win situation in my relationship.

5. I give all my errors to the Holy Spirit for correction, keeping none. I let go of all values I held that are inappropriate. I give each problem to the Holy Spirit for solution.

6. I know that, to the Holy Spirit, everything justifies forgiveness, therefore I am forgiven and free. The Holy Spirit can commute each sentence I laid upon myself into a blessing.

7. I do not have to lose for anyone to gain. They do not have to lose for me to gain.

8. I have gratitude for God's justice. Salvation is God's justice.

9. The miracle I receive I give. I offer peace to all.

On a separate piece of paper, make a list of your own applications.

During the ten days you are studying Chapter Twenty-Five in the Text, learn one lesson a day in the workbook, summarizing what you learned in this space.

Day 241: _____

Day 242: _____

Day 243: _____

Day 244: _____

Day 245: _____

Day 246: _____

Day 247: _____

Day 248: _____

Day 249: _____

Day 250: _____

Chapter Twenty=Six

Now you are shifting back and forth between the past and present. The only value the past can hold is that you learn it gave you no rewards. He who lives in memories is unaware of where he is. He cannot go back nor can he lose the way. The way to Heaven's Gate is not difficult at all. There is a borderland of thought that stands between the world and heaven. It is not a place. It is a meeting where thoughts are brought together. Here is every thought made pure.

Think how great your release will be when you are willing to receive correction for all your problems! If God is just, then there can be no problems that justice cannot solve. Each time you keep a problem for yourself to solve, or judge that it is one that has no resolution, you have made it great and past hope of healing. Your problem will recur and then recur again and yet again, until it has been answered for all time. The Holy Spirit offers you release from every problem you think you have. It has no greater difficulty in resolving some than others. Every problem is just an error to the Holy Spirit.

In order for the purpose of the *Course* to be accepted, you must understand the laws of healing. Here are the principles:

1. All sickness came from separation. When separation is denied, the sickness goes.

2. No illusion has any truth in it, even though it may appear to you that some are more true than others. This makes no sense at all.

3. Sins are beliefs you impose between others and yourself. They limit

you to time and place. Forgiveness takes away what stands between you. There is no sin.

4. Every miracle is possible the instant you perceive that your wishes and the will of God are one. What is God's will? He wills his Son have everything, and this He guaranteed when He created Him as everything!

5. From the error that attack can be projected outside the mind, a world of sin and sacrifice arose. (This world is an attempt to prove your innocence while cherishing attack.)

6. Cause and effect are one. When cause and consequence are brought together, the miracle is possible. The healing of effect without cause is not release.

7. In every wish to hurt, you chose death. You have, however, been given power to save the Son of God from crucifixion, hell and death.

Salvation is immediate. Delay is senseless. Your mistake is thinking there is an interval of time between when you forgive and trusting your brother. Do not forget that a shadow held between your brother and you obscures the face of Christ and the memory of God.

Would you trade them for an ancient hate? Where an ancient hate has become a present love is one of the holiest of all the spots on earth.

You have no enemy but yourself. Beware of the temptation to perceive yourself as unfairly treated. Each unfairness that the world appears to lay upon you, you have laid upon it. Do not deny the presence of the holy angels by such beliefs.

The holy angels hover over you to keep away all darkness and hold the light where it has entered. Welcome them!

Examples of Applications for Chapter Twenty-Six

1. I am willing to receive correction for all my problems. There is not one for which I cannot get a solution if I give it to the Holy Spirit.

2. I do not imagine that one illusion is true. None of them are true.

3. I do not impose sin on my sisters and brothers, nor limit them to a body. I am careful not to sacrifice my oneness by seeing my brother or sister in another body, apart from mine.

4. My wishes are the same as the will of God. God wills that I have everything. This is natural, since he created me as everything.

5. I cannot project attack outside of my mind. I am at cause and my mind causes effects.

6. It is natural for me to use the power God has given me.

7. I accept salvation and happiness now. There is no reason to delay.

8. I cannot be unfairly treated. People treat me the way I treat myself. The way I treat a brother is my opinion of myself. God is in my brother. I always regard him gently.

9. I am willing to have all my relationships totally cleaned up. I do not allow any ancient hatred to come between me and any other person.

10. I welcome the angels and do not interfere with their help.

On a separate piece of paper, make a list of your own applications.

During the ten days you are studying Chapter Twenty-Six
in the Text, learn one lesson a day in the workbook,
summarizing what you learned in this space.

Day 251: _____

Day 252: _____

Day 253: _____

Day 254: _____

Day 255: _____

Day 256: _____

Day 257: _____

Day 258: _____

Day 259: _____

Day 260: _____

Chapter Twenty=Seven

The dreamer sees himself attacked unjustly and by something not himself. He is a "victim" of this "something else." (Suffering is an emphasis upon all that the world has done to you.) The dreamer thinks he must be innocent because he doesn't notice what he does, but only what is done to him. He cannot escape because the source is seen outside himself.

Every pain you suffer, you see as proof that someone else is guilty. To you sickness is the witness to that guilt and death proves the errors must be sins. This is the picture of your crucifixion. The sick remain accusers. A broken body shows the mind has not been healed. Pain compels attention, drawing it away from Him, focusing on itself. A body carries the message that you can be hurt.

The body is the central figure of the dreaming of the world. It tells the story of how it was made by other bodies, born into a world outside the body, lives a little while and dies to be united in dust with other dying bodies. In the brief time allotted to live, it searches for other bodies and safety is its main concern. It looks about the "special" bodies that can share its dream. Sometimes it dreams it is a conqueror of bodies weaker than itself.

The Holy Spirit pictures a different you. It is a picture of a different body, one that has not been used to attack and therefore never suffered pain at all. The Holy Spirit takes away from the body all signs of accusation and blame. It is pictured without a purpose. Your body stands waiting for its purpose to be given.

In this empty space heaven is free to be remembered. Here, peace can come and perfect healing takes the place of death. The body can become a sign of life, a promise of redemption, a breath of Immortality. Let the body have no purpose from the past. Let it receive the power to represent an endless life forever unattacked.

The only way to heal is to be healed. Health is the witness to health. The only thing that is required for healing is a *lack of fear*. The fearful are not healed and cannot be healed.

God has given you a way of reaching another state of mind and that has transcended conflict and reached toward peace. Come to the Holy Instant and be healed; being blessed, you will bring blessing. Life is given you to give the dying world. The Holy Instant's radiance will light your eyes, giving them ability to see beyond all suffering to Christ's face. Healing replaces suffering.

There is no need to suffer any more, but there is a need to be healed. Bring all forms of suffering to Him and He will teach you how each one is caused. The secret of salvation is this: That you are doing this to yourself.

The resurrection of the world awaits your healing and your happiness, that you may demonstrate the healing of the world.

Examples of Applications for Chapter Twenty-Seven

1. I confess that I have been asleep and living in a dream, acting like a victim, making my brother and the world to blame.

2. Accusing others or something outside of me makes me sick. When my body is sick and broken down it is because my mind is off.

3. I no longer use pain and illness as a way to distract myself from God. Where the pain and disease are, that is where I am hanging onto the ego and making it real. I did this to myself.

4. My emphasis on the body and its protection is inappropriate. I don't even know what the true purpose of the body is. I do not give it purposes of the past. I give it no purpose, waiting for its purpose to be given.

5. I accept the miracle of healing for myself and allow myself to be completely healed. I offer others what I have received. My health inspires others to be healthy.

6. I now let go of all fear of healing. I transcend any remaining conflict, and I come to the holy instant to be healed.

7. I receive as much life as possible and give life to others. I am part of the resurrection now.

8. I apply what I have learned to myself and teach others what I have learned.

On a separate piece of paper, make a list of your own applications.

*During the ten days you are studying Chapter Twenty-Seven
in the Text, learn one lesson a day in the workbook,
summarizing what you learned in this space.*

Day 261: _____

Day 262: _____

Day 263: _____

Day 264: _____

Day 265: _____

Day 266: _____

Day 267: _____

Day 268: _____

Day 269: _____

Day 270: _____

NOTE

Remember Nothing that You Taught Yourself
for
You Were Badly Taught

Chapter Twenty-Eight

If you are a dreamer, at least perceive this much: *You have caused the dream you do not like.* You have put yourself to sleep. Before you can change the content, you must realize it is you who created the dream. When you see that you are author of your dreams, your fear can leave. The fear is held in place and will be there as long as you see the dream in another's hands. Remember, you are not a victim.

Sickness is a dream where you punish yourself. Sickness is a sense of limitation, a splitting off and separating from, a gap seen between yourself and health. It is a separating from good and embracing evil. Sickness is anger taken out on the body so that it will suffer pain. Who punishes the body is insane.

The body only does what it is told. It behaves the way you want, but *it* never makes the choice. If you think the body causes your pain, you have confused cause and effect. This is the separation's final step. The body is an effect. Effects do not create their cause.

The cause of pain is separation, not the body. You send the body forth to seek separation and be a separate thing, then hate it for the uses you have made of it. You despise its acts but not your own. It seems to punish you, yet you are the one who has made it a symbol of the limitations you want to keep. You think the body is yourself and without it you'd be lost.

Who can build a home upon straw and count on it as shelter from the wind? The body is like this because it lacks foundation in truth.

Like you, your brother thinks he is a dream. Do not give support to his dream of sickness and death. Do not share his wish to separate

159

and turn illusions on himself. Unless you help him, you will suffer pain with him. If you are part of others' fearful dreams, you will lose identity in them. *Do not allow your brother to be sick,* for if he is, you have abandoned him to his own dream by sharing it with him.

Uniting with another's true mind prevents the cause of sickness and its perceived effects. (The mind cannot project its guilt without your aid.) You stand apart from your sister's dreams but not from her. You share no evil dreams if you forgive the dreams. The beautiful relationship you have with all your brothers and sisters is part of you because it is part of God Himself. What is joined cannot be separate.

God is the alternative to dreams of fear. Where fear has gone, there love must come. Don't be afraid, but let your world be lit by miracles. The door is open that all those who come in may no longer starve, but enjoy the feast of plenty. There is an unlimited supply. No one is deprived or can deprive. The more anyone receives, the more is left for all the rest to share.

The mind that has no fear instantly remembers God, and in God's memory offers all its treasures.

Examples of Applications for Chapter Twenty-Eight

1. I am the author of my dreams. I caused what I don't like.

2. It is up to me to change the dream by changing my thoughts.

3. My body is an effect of my mind. My mind rules my body—therefore all illness is mental illness. Since I created my sickness, I can also uncreate it.

4. Since I was the thinker whose negative thoughts made me sick, I am also the thinker who can think thoughts that make me well. (All pain is the effort involved in clinging to a negative thought.)

5. The old purpose for which I used my body resulted in a weak foundation. I need a new purpose.

6. I let the Holy Spirit teach me the purpose. I use my body now as an aid to reaching home to God. My body can also serve to help the healing of God's Son.

7. I do not go into agreement with the negative thoughts and illnesses of others. I do not match energies with them if they are negative or sick.

8. At a time like that, I inspire others to remember who they are. I see them whole and healed, and strengthen that in them.

9. Fear is the ego. The ego is not real. There is nothing to fear.

10. God is all that I want. God is love. God is life. God is opulence and infinite supply. God is everlasting immortality.

On a separate piece of paper, make a list of your own applications.

D*uring the ten days you are studying Chapter Twenty-Eight*
in the Text, learn one lesson a day in the workbook,
summarizing what you learned in this space.

Day 271: _____

Day 272: _____

Day 273: _____

Day 274: _____

Day 275: _____

Day 276: _____

Day 277: _____

Day 278: _____

Day 279: _____

Day 280: _____

Chapter Twenty=Nine

Love is treacherous to those who fear, since fear and hate are never apart. No one hates unless afraid of love, and thus afraid of God. When you fear to love and love to hate, you think that love is fearful and hate is love. It is not that love demands sacrifice, but that fear demands sacrifice of love. *In love's presence fear cannot abide.*

The fear of God: The great obstacle is not yet gone.

Every dream (illusion) is a dream of fear, no matter what the form. Depression and assault are made of fear. The choice is not between which dreams to keep—you are either sleeping or awake. Nightmares are childish dreams wherein the toys have turned against the child. Put away the toys of children, you need them no more.

The body will allow only limited indulgences in love. It will command when to love and when to shrink away from love. Yet it is you who endowed it with power it does not have—power over you. Now it tells you where to go and how; it dictates what it can tolerate and what will make it sick. It will be sick because you do not know what loving means.

Sickness is a demand that the body be a thing that it is not. (Its nothingness is a guarantee that it cannot be sick.) You demanded it be more than nothing. You asked it to be God's enemy and therefore it will be attacked. You went so far as to perceive death as life! Confusion follows confusion in your mind.

How much do you desire peace instead of endless strife and misery?

Swear not to die! Don't think you can set a goal unlike God's purpose for you. You were not born to die. Life's function cannot be to die. Life's function is life's extension. You are as immortal as your Father. This world will bind your feet, tie your hands and kill your body *only* if you think it was made to crucify God's Son.

Do you prefer to be right or happy?

The world of idols is a veil across the face of Christ. Idols are substitutes for your reality. (Sickness, misery, depression, pain, suffering and death are idols.) An idol is a false impression or belief, the purpose of which is to conceal the truth from you. You do not understand that the idol you seek is your death.

Whenever you fear in any form—and you are fearful if you do not feel deep content, certainty of help, and calm assurance that heaven goes with you—be sure you have made an idol and it will betray you.

The fear of God is the fear of loss of idols.

The promise of the loving God is that his Son have life and every living thing be part of Him. There is no change in immortality. There is no death because the living share the function their Creator gave to them. Life's function is that it be as one forever and ever without end. The changelessness of heaven is in you. The still infinity of endless peace surrounds you gently in its soft embrace.

Your Guest has come. You asked Him and He came. You did not hear Him enter because you did not wholly welcome Him, and yet his gifts came with Him. Why are you not rejoicing?

Examples of Applications for Chapter Twenty-Nine

1. I separate fear from love. I pray to give up all my fear of love.

2. The more I give up illusions the less fear I will have.

3. My body does not have power over me. I am in charge of my body and I do not use it inappropriately.

4. Death is not God's goal for me. The purpose of the world is *not* to crucify me. There is nothing outside of me that can kill me.

5. I no longer worship the idols of sin, suffering, pain and death. Forgive me for putting these false gods before you. I was wrong.

6. Immortality is reality. I rejoice that I am free!

On a separate piece of paper, make a list of your own applications.

D*uring the ten days you are studying Chapter Twenty-Nine*
in the Text, learn one lesson a day in the workbook,
summarizing what you learned in this space.

Day 281: _____

Day 282: _____

Day 283: _____

Day 284: _____

Day 285: _____

Day 286: _____

Day 287: _____

Day 288: _____

Day 289: _____

Day 290: _____

Chapter Thirty

You must go beyond idols to get the new beginning. But the purpose of an idol is to limit you. Decide for idols and you ask for less.

Behind the search for every idol lies the yearning for completion. Completion is the function of God's Son. It is God's will that everything be yours. You do not want whatever you believe an idol gives. Illusions bring fear because they hide the truth. You will always attack what doesn't satisfy you to avoid seeing that you made it up. But attack has no foundation and anger is never justified. Pardon is always justified.

Salvation asks that you respond appropriately to what is not real by not perceiving what has not occurred. It is a paradox: It asks that you forgive all things that no one ever did, to overlook what is not there, and not to look upon the unreal as reality.

The real world is the state of mind in which the only purpose of the world is seen to be forgiveness.

To reach a new beginning, your willingness to practice each step is imperative. If you find your dedication is weak, and your resistance is strong, you are *not ready*. Don't fight your self.

(It is important to see that you still make up your mind and *then* decide to ask what you should do. But your decisions are made with idols and you ask the Antichrist for help.)

Rules for Decision

1. The outlook starts with this: Today I will make no decision by myself. With this outlook you are not the judge of what you do. When you are called upon to make a response, you do not judge the situations.

2. Tell yourself the kind of day you want, the feelings you want to have, the things you want to happen and what you want to experience. Then realize: *This is the day that will be given me if I make no decisions myself.*

3. If something occurred in your day that is not what you wanted, realize that you have asked a question by yourself in the ego. Then say: *I have no questions. I forgot to decide.*

4. If you cannot let your questions go, begin to change your mind with this: *At least I can decide I do not like what I feel now.*

5. Having decided that you do not like the way you feel, the next step is easy: *I hope I have been wrong.* (This reminds you help is what you want and need. Now you've reached the turning point.)

6. You can say now in perfect honesty: *I want another way to look at this.*

7. The final step is an acknowledgement of your lack of opposition. It is a statement of an open mind: *Perhaps there is another way to look at this. What can I lose by asking?*

Decisions cause results. They are made by you and your adviser. Who is your adviser, Christ or the ego? If you oppose the Holy Spirit you fight yourself.

The Holy Spirit tells you your will. He speaks for you. God asks you to do your will and he joins with you. How wonderful it is to do your will, for that is freedom. Your will is boundless.

The happy dream is perfect health, perfect freedom from all forms of lack, and safety from disaster of all kinds. There is no miracle you cannot have when you desire healing.

Examples of Applications for Chapter Thirty

1. When I choose an idol I am asking for less. I am saying I have no need for everything. I must remember that idols will not satisfy me and that it is my will to have everything.

2. I do not limit myself by making idols . . . nor do I attack something that does not satisfy me. (This is just a way to avoid seeing that I created it.) I no longer make up things that don't satisfy me.

3. There is no justification for my anger because I made up everything that makes me angry.

4. I choose salvation and a new beginning.

    a. I make no decisions by myself.

    b. The less I decide by myself, the more I get what I want.

    c. When things don't go right or I feel bad, it is because I decided with the Antichrist (ego). I had a negative thought I was trying to prove.

    d. I do not want to continue feeling bad.

    e. I admit that I have been wrong.

    f. I want a new way.

    g. I am totally open to a new way. I have nothing to lose.

5. My adviser now is the Holy Spirit.

6. I now create perfect freedom, perfect health, abundance and safety. Immortality is mine. I want and accept healing and miracles.

On a separate piece of paper, make a list of your own applications.

*During the ten days you are studying Chapter Thirty
in the Text, learn one lesson a day in the workbook,
summarizing what you learned in this space.*

Day 291: _____

Day 292: _____

Day 293: _____

Day 294: _____

Day 295: _____

Day 296: _____

Day 297: _____

Day 298: _____

Day 299: _____

Day 300: _____

Chapter Thirty=One

There are only two lessons to be learned. Each has its outcome in a different world. Which lesson will you learn?

First lesson: *That God's Son is guilty.*
>The outcome of that lesson is the world that you see: a world of terror and despair. In it no plan for safety will succeed.

Second lesson: *That God's Son is innocent.*
>The outcome of this lesson is a world in which there is no fear and everything is lit with hope and sparkles with a gentle friendliness.

Temptation is a wish to make the wrong decision.
BE STILL AN INSTANT AND FORGET ALL THE THINGS YOU EVER LEARNED!

Then learn this: Only the self-accused condemn. You can never hate your brother for his sins, only for your own. Why are his sins real in him if you did not believe they are in you?

You can change what you believe. The body will follow.

There is a tendency to think the world can offer consolation and escape from problems that its purpose is to keep. All its roads lead to disappointment, nothingness and death. There is no hope of answers in the world. Look no longer for hope where there is none. Happiness cannot be found by following a road away from it.

The concept of the self has always been the great preoccupation of the world. The concept of the self is made by you and bears no likeness to your self at all. It is an idol made to take the place of your reality as God's child. Salvation can be seen as an escape from concepts. To clear yourself, say "I do not know the thing I am and therefore do not know what I am doing, where I am, or how to look upon the world myself." Start with a clean slate.

You always have the choice to see the flesh or recognize the spirit. If you choose to see the body, you behold a world of separation. This appears and disappears in death, doomed to suffering and loss. ARE YOU A BODY?

Choose the spirit and all heaven bends to touch your eyes and bless your holy sight. ARE YOU SPIRIT? Deathless, without corruption? Then you see the world as stable, worthy of your trust, a happy place.

What is temptation but the wish to stay in misery? There is hell or heaven, and you can choose only one.

CHOOSE AGAIN. Bring your weakness unto Him and He will give you strength. You are as God created you and so is every living thing you look upon.

Examples of Applications for Chapter Thirty-One

1. I learn the lesson now that I am not guilty.

2. The more I see my own innocence and that of others, the more I am free of fear and see a friendly world.

3. If I see sins in others, they are mine.

4. My body does not think. If it gets sick and dies it is because my mind is sick.

5. I can change what I believe and my body follows.

6. I do not find happiness by looking at the world. The world does not offer me salvation, so I stop looking there. It is a waste of time.

7. I give up all self-concepts.

8. I choose not to see myself or others as a body.

9. I am Spirit and deathless (since Spirit is that which cannot be destroyed).

10. I choose heaven, knowing that it is a decision I must make.

11. I am as God created me, perfect like He is, immortal like He is.

On a separate piece of paper, make a list of your own applications.

During the ten days you are studying Chapter Thirty-One
in the Text, learn one lesson a day in the workbook,
summarizing what you learned in this space.

Day 301: _____

Day 302: _____

Day 303: _____

Day 304: _____

Day 305: _____

Day 306: _____

Day 307: _____

Day 308: _____

Day 309: _____

Day 310: _____

What is Forgiveness?

Forgiveness recognizes that what you thought your brother did to you has not occurred. It does not pardon sins and make them real; it sees there was no sin. In that view all your sins are forgiven.

Sin is a false idea about God's Son. Forgiveness merely sees its falsity and therefore lets it go. (An unforgiving thought is one which makes a judgment. The mind is closed and will not be released. An unforgiving thought has distortion as its purpose.)

God has forgiven you already, for such is His function. You share His function.

What is Salvation?

Salvation is a promise made by God that you will find your way to Him at last. It will be kept. God's Word replaces thoughts of conflict with thoughts of peace. (The thought of peace was given to God's Son the instant his mind had the thought of war.)

Salvation lets illusions go, not supporting them. And what was hidden is now revealed: an altar to the Holy Name of God. The memory of God is not far behind. In this holy place there is no sorrow. Earth is born again in new perspective. We come together in the light. Freedom is returned and we are rejoicing.

GO ON WITH THE NEXT TEN LESSONS. During these next ten days discuss the *Course* with people you know or meet. Attempt to talk to at least one person a day about *A Course in Miracles*. (The *Course* says repeatedly that we must take all our brothers with us to complete God's plan for salvation.) Tell people about the books, show them the books, share what you got out of them and explain how to get them—or give sets away. Write up your experiences below and continue to study one lesson daily.

Day 1: Names of people I shared with and my experience with them:

Day 2: Names of people I shared with and my experience with them:

Day 3: Names of people I shared with and my experience with them:

Day 4: Names of people I shared with and my experience with them:

Day 5: Names of people I shared with and my experience with them:

Day 6: Names of people I shared with and my experience with them:

Day 7: Names of people I shared with and my experience with them:

Day 8: Names of people I shared with and my experience with them:

Day 9: Names of people I shared with and my experience with them:

Day 10: Names of people I shared with and my experience with them:

During these ten days when you are sharing with people about the Course, learn one lesson a day, summarizing it in this space.

Day 311: _____

Day 312: _____

Day 313: _____

Day 314: _____

Day 315: _____

Day 316: _____

Day 317: _____

Day 318: _____

Day 319: _____

Day 320: _____

187

What Is the World?

The world is a false perception, born of error. When the thought of separation has been changed to one of true forgiveness, the world will be seen in quite another light. This world was made as an attack on God and symbolizes fear. Since fear is love's absence, this world was meant to be a place where God could not enter and the Son of God could be apart.

A perception that leads away from the truth can be redirected. Perception can be given a new purpose by the One whom God appointed as Savior. Follow His Light and see the world as He beholds it. We must save the world by beholding it through the eyes of Christ. What was made to die can be restored to everlasting life.

What Is Sin?

Sin is insanity. It is the means by which the mind is driven mad, and seeks to let illusions take the place of truth. Sin is the home of all illusions. Sin "proves" God's Son is evil, that timelessness must have an end, eternal life must die, and God Himself has lost the Son He loves. This is insane.

Sin appears to terrify—a madman's dreams *are* frightening. It is all a childish game. The Son of God can pretend He has become a body, prey to evil, guilt and death, but all the while God shines on Him and loves Him. *There is no sin.* Creation is unchanged. How long will you maintain the game of sin?

GO ON WITH THE NEXT TEN LESSONS. During these next ten days discuss the *Course* with people you know or meet. Attempt to talk to at least one person a day about *A Course in Miracles*. (The *Course* says repeatedly that we must take all our brothers with us to complete God's plan for salvation.) Tell people about the books, show them the books, share what you got out of them and explain how to get them—or give sets away. Write up your experiences below and continue to study one lesson daily.

Day 1: Names of people I shared with and my experience with them:

Day 2: Names of people I shared with and my experience with them:

Day 3: Names of people I shared with and my experience with them:

Day 4: Names of people I shared with and my experience with them:

Day 5: Names of people I shared with and my experience with them:

Day 6: Names of people I shared with and my experience with them:

Day 7: Names of people I shared with and my experience with them:

Day 8: Names of people I shared with and my experience with them:

Day 9: Names of people I shared with and my experience with them·

Day 10: Names of people I shared with and my experience with them:

During these ten days when you are sharing with people about the Course, *learn one lesson a day, summarizing it in this space.*

Day 321: _____

Day 322: _____

Day 323: _____

Day 324: _____

Day 325: _____

Day 326: _____

Day 327: _____

Day 328: _____

Day 329: _____

Day 330: _____

What Is the Body?

The body is a fence you imagine you have built to separate part of your self from the other parts. You think you live within this fence to decay, crumble and die. But the body is a dream which will melt and fade away (dematerialize) when Christ is made manifest.

We can change the purpose of the body by changing what we think it is for. It was a place to hide from love in the pursuit of hell. It can be a means by which God's Son returns to sanity with the goal of heaven. Extending your hand to others on this path while using the body to heal the mind makes it holy. *Love is your safety,* not the body.

What Is the Christ?

Christ is God's Son, the link that keeps you one with God. Your mind is part of His and His of yours. He has not left his holy home and abides forever unchanged in the mind of God. In Him God placed the means for your salvation.

Home of the Holy Spirit, He unites us with God and with one another. The Christ in you does not inhabit a body, because wholeness is unlimited and has no form. Yet *He is in you.* The Holy Spirit reaches from the Christ in you, exchanging all your dreams for the final one God appointed as the end of all dreams. Let us seek to find His face and nothing else.

GO ON WITH THE NEXT TEN LESSONS. During these next ten days discuss the *Course* with people you know or meet. Attempt to talk to at least one person a day about *A Course in Miracles.* (The *Course* says repeatedly that we must take all our brothers with us to complete God's plan for salvation.) Tell people about the books, show them the books, share what you got out of them and explain how to get them—or give sets away. Write up your experiences below and continue to study one lesson daily.

Day 1: Names of people I shared with and my experience with them:

Day 2: Names of people I shared with and my experience with them:

Day 3: Names of people I shared with and my experience with them:

Day 4: Names of people I shared with and my experience with them:

Day 5: Names of people I shared with and my experience with them:

Day 6: Names of people I shared with and my experience with them:

Day 7: Names of people I shared with and my experience with them:

Day 8: Names of people I shared with and my experience with them:

Day 9: Names of people I shared with and my experience with them:

Day 10: Names of people I shared with and my experience with them:

During these ten days when you are sharing with people about
the Course, *learn one lesson a day, summarizing it in this space.*

Day 331: _____

Day 332: _____

Day 333: _____

Day 334: _____

Day 335: _____

Day 336: _____

Day 337: _____

Day 338: _____

Day 339: _____

Day 340: _____

201

What Is the Holy Spirit?

The Holy Spirit is the voice for God. It mediates between illusions and truth. It provides the bridge where all dreams are carried to truth. Its goal is the end of all dreams. The Holy Spirit is described throughout the *Course* as resolving the separation and bringing us the plan of the Atonement. It establishes Jesus as the leader in carrying out God's plan, since Jesus was the first to complete his own part perfectly.

The Holy Spirit is the remaining communication link between God and His separated Sons. It never forgets you. It is God's gift. It restores sanity and peace of mind. Accept your Father's gift and it will restore the quietness of Heaven to you.

What Is the Real World?

The real world is opposite to what you made. It is perceived through eyes of forgiveness instead of fear. It is a correction for fear and battle.

In the real world there are no cries of pain and sorrow, no thoughts of attack, murder and death. Sin and guilt are gone. There is no danger of any kind. Only happy sights and sounds can reach your mind. There is only safety, love and joy. There is no need for time. The mind is at peace with itself and there is only kindness.

GO ON WITH THE NEXT TEN LESSONS. During these next ten days discuss the *Course* with people you know or meet. Attempt to talk to at least one person a day about *A Course in Miracles*. (The *Course* says repeatedly that we must take all our brothers with us to complete God's plan for salvation.) Tell people about the books, show them the books, share what you got out of them and explain how to get them—or give sets away. Write up your experiences below and continue to study one lesson daily.

Day 1: Names of people I shared with and my experience with them:

Day 2: Names of people I shared with and my experience with them:

Day 3: Names of people I shared with and my experience with them:

.Day 4: Names of people I shared with and my experience with them:

Day 5: Names of people I shared with and my experience with them:

Day 6: Names of people I shared with and my experience with them:

Day 7: Names of people I shared with and my experience with them:

Day 8: Names of people I shared with and my experience with them:

Day 9: Names of people I shared with and my experience with them:

Day 10: Names of people I shared with and my experience with them:

During these ten days when you are sharing with people about the Course, learn one lesson a day, summarizing it in this space.

Day 341: _____

Day 342: _____

Day 343: _____

Day 344: _____

Day 345: _____

Day 346: _____

Day 347: _____

Day 348: _____

Day 349: _____

Day 350: _____

What Is the Second Coming?

The Second Coming is merely the correction of mistakes and the return to Sanity. It is as sure as God.

The Second Coming ends the lessons that the Holy Spirit teaches. All minds are given to the hands of Christ. The Second Coming is the end of the ego's rule.

Pray that the Second Coming is soon. It needs your total willingness.

What Is the Last Judgment?

The Last Judgment contains *no condemnation*. It sees the world as totally forgiven. (The Voice of God proclaims what is false, and what is true has never changed.) The world is seen as without sin and purposeless. His judgment is not hell. It is the return to peace, security, happiness and union.

This is the final judgment:

You are still my Holy Son. Forever innocent, forever loving and forever loved, as limitless as your Creator, completely changeless and forever pure.

GO ON WITH THE NEXT TEN LESSONS. During these next ten days discuss the *Course* with people you know or meet. Attempt to talk to at least one person a day about *A Course in Miracles*. (The *Course* says repeatedly that we must take all our brothers with us to complete God's plan for salvation.) Tell people about the books, show them the books, share what you got out of them and explain how to get them—or give sets away. Write up your experiences below and continue to study one lesson daily.

Day 1: Names of people I shared with and my experience with them:

Day 2: Names of people I shared with and my experience with them:

Day 3: Names of people I shared with and my experience with them:

Day 4: Names of people I shared with and my experience with them:

Day 5: Names of people I shared with and my experience with them:

Day 6: Names of people I shared with and my experience with them:

Day 7: Names of people I shared with and my experience with them:

Day 8: Names of people I shared with and my experience with them:

Day 9: Names of people I shared with and my experience with them:

Day 10: Names of people I shared with and my experience with them:

During these ten days when you are sharing with people about
the Course, learn one lesson a day, summarizing it in this space.

Day 351: _____

Day 352: _____

Day 353: _____

Day 354: _____

Day 355: _____

Day 356: _____

Day 357: _____

Day 358: _____

Day 359: _____

Day 360: _____

215

What Is Creation?

Creation is the sum of all God's thoughts—in number infinite, and everywhere without limit. Only love creates, and only like itself. His Son shares in creation and must therefore share in power to create.

Creation is the truth. It is the opposite of all illusions. We are creation. We are the Son of God. In creation is His will complete in every aspect. Oneness is guaranteed.

What Is the Ego?

The ego is the negative thoughts we made up about the self. The ego is idolatry, the sign of the limited and separated self, born in a body, doomed to suffer and die. It sees the will of God as enemy. To the ego, strength is weak, love is fearful, life is death and what opposes God is true. The ego is insane. It thinks it has become a victor over God Himself.

To know reality is *not* to see the ego and its thoughts, its works, its acts, its laws, its beliefs and its dreams. The Son of God is egoless because the ego is not real.

The ego offers you crucifixion. The ego is a thing of madness. The ego is nothingness, not reality at all.

GO ON WITH THE NEXT TEN LESSONS. During these next ten days discuss the *Course* with people you know or meet. Attempt to talk to at least one person a day about *A Course in Miracles*. (The *Course* says repeatedly that we must take all our brothers with us to complete God's plan for salvation.) Tell people about the books, show them the books, share what you got out of them and explain how to get them—or give sets away. Write up your experiences below and continue to study one lesson daily.

Day 1: Names of people I shared with and my experience with them:

Day 2: Names of people I shared with and my experience with them:

Day 3: Names of people I shared with and my experience with them:

Day 4: Names of people I shared with and my experience with them:

Day 5: Names of people I shared with and my experience with them:

Day 6: Names of people I shared with and my experience with them:

Day 7: Names of people I shared with and my experience with them·

Day 8: Names of people I shared with and my experience with them·

Day 9: Names of people I shared with and my experience with them:

Day 10: Names of people I shared with and my experience with them:

During these last five days when you are sharing with people about the Course, *continue to learn this last lesson, summarizing it in this space.*

Day 361: _____

Day 362: _____

Day 363: _____

Day 364: _____

Day 365: _____

What Is a Miracle?

A Miracle is correction. It does not create, it undoes error. It contains the gift of grace. Forgiveness is the home of miracles. The ego's opposite in every way is what we call a miracle.

The miracle is taken first on faith. No miracle is withheld from anyone. The miracle forgives. Miracles fall like drops of healing rain from heaven on a dry and dusty world where starved and thirsty creatures come to die. Now they have water. Signs of life spring up, and what has life has immortality.

What Am I?

I am God's child, complete and healed, whole, shining in the reflection of His love. In me is His creation. In me is love perfected and joy established. I am the holy home of God Himself. I am the heaven where His love resides.

Through my eyes Christ's vision sees a world redeemed from every thought of sin. Through my ears the voice for God is heard proclaiming the world as sinless. Our minds join together as we bless the world.

We are holy messengers for God, the bringers of Salvation. We accept our part as Saviors of the world.

221

Afterword

Congratulations on completing your first year with the *Course*. Now you can start all over. In the second year the *Course* seems a lot easier, more fun, more rewarding and more understandable because your ego will have less rule.

This course is a beginning, not an end. Your friend, the Holy Spirit, goes with you. You are not alone. No one who calls on Him calls in vain. Whatever troubles you, be certain that He has the answer and will gladly give it to you. All you have to do is turn to Him and ask for it. He gives only the eternal and the good. Let Him prepare you further.

Solution

The Holy Spirit is God's answer to the ego. He brings the plan of the Atonement and leads us back to our real self. The Atonement (Atonement with God) is the complete removal of guilt. The holy instant allows the Holy Spirit's correction to occur. It is the miracle of instantaneous forgiveness.

To the Holy Spirit the world is a place that provides opportunities to forgive. People are seen as either acting out of love or calling for love. The Second Coming of Christ is the end of the ego's rule.

However, right before the fear (ego) is transcended the ego screams Stop! You do not want the separation healed! You must be vigilant against this temptation.

In the Bible, Revelation says that Jesus stands at the door and knocks. Our fear is *not* that, when we open the door, Christ won't be there; our fear is that He will! For in His presence the ego's world is dispelled. All fear and guilt are gone.

Very often we have asked for God's help in removing a problem. Help never came and we became very disappointed and thought there was no God. It is not that God wasn't there or that God refused our request, however, but that we did not ask clearly. While we were asking for a problem resolved, the ego's voice was urging us to hold on to it. In other words, we were giving a double message. Example: You may have prayed for something you deserve but at the same time you had a subconscious thought (Personal Law) like "I can't get what I want" or "I'm not good enough" that was so strong it sabotaged your receiving anything. If your fear of letting go of those thoughts is too great, God will wait. The Holy Spirit will not add to your fear.

When you develop a consciousness of the things you seek, they will appear in your presence. God meets you on the level of your consciousness. If your consciousness of need is greater than your consciousness of God, then need will expand. When you love God more than your problem, you will be healed. You must rededicate your self. You must develop the state of mind through which you can receive God.

Prayer is a way to clear the way for your acceptance of your oneness with the Source. (The stream has the quality of its source.) You must pray from the standpoint of already having what you ask for (knowing there is no spiritual lack.) Prayer is the practice of the presence of God.

1. Lay hold of the good you desire.

2. Recognize it is here now.

3. Have absolute confidence.

4. Express gratitude.

Give thanks instead of complaining, fearing or worrying. A thankful mind attracts good.

When you identify yourself with the truth of your Being, life can never be disappointing or unproductive again. Your life, your power, your health and your happiness depend on your acceptance of God. Your spiritual self must come forth. The problem is you forgot that the Creator and the created are one.

But what is God? you might ask. God is beyond definition. Any definition would limit God. God is unlimited. *I am that I am* means: "I am unlimited potential." That is what you are: unlimited potential.

In Summary

(Thank You, Ken Wapnick)

The *Course* describes the post-separated self at war against God. The following will remind you of this descent into hell and inspire you to choose against it.

EGO

A false self we constructed to replace God. A decision to remain separate. Comes from the thought "I am not."

GUILT

We therefore have tremendous guilt about this "crime."

FEAR of PUNISHMENT

We are sure we will be punished and God is seen as an avenger.

GOD of LOVE BECOMES GOD of FEAR

AVOIDING GOD

FEAR LEADS to INCREASED GUILT

INCREASED GUILT INTENSIFIES FEAR

INTENSE FEAR of GOD OCCURS

FEAR WE WILL BE STRUCK DEAD by GOD

BASIC ANXIETY

Feeling of unworthiness, inadequacy, inferiority, leading to the beliefs: "I don't deserve life," "I am not of the Father and cannot share in His peace, joy and happiness," or "I should be dead."

FEAR of GOD INCREASES and THEREFORE
DESIRE to REMAIN SEPARATE from HIM INCREASES

NEED for PROTECTION INCREASES

Constant vigilance against the fear reinforces it.

DEFENSES

Consequences get devastating—war, bombs, etc.

GUILT INTENSIFIES BELIEF THAT GUILT CAN NEVER BE UNDONE

Sin is seen as unredeemable.

NO HOPE

BELIEF THAT GUILT CAN BE REMOVED ONLY by
PROJECTION ONTO SOMETHING EXTERNAL

PROJECTION

*We project onto the world the judgment of ourselves as
fearful, guilty, deprived and separate.*

WORLD IS SEEN as PLACE of CONDEMNATION

Hell.

The ego's plan for salvation is a false solution. It consists of making defenses. This is like sweeping the problem under the rug.

Seven Aspects of God

1. GOD IS LIFE   (Joy is the highest expression of God and Life.)

2. GOD IS TRUTH   (To know the truth about any condition heals it.)

3. GOD IS LOVE   (When you love God more than your problem you will be healed.)

4. GOD IS INTELLIGENCE   (When you realize this, the old beliefs will be overcome.)

5. GOD IS SOUL   (That aspect by which He is able to individualize.)

6. GOD IS SPIRIT   (That which cannot be destroyed. If you realize you are one with spirit, you cannot be destroyed and immortality is obvious.)

7. GOD IS PRINCIPLE   (Example: perfect harmony. God does not change.)

(I thank Unity Church, The Church of Religious Science, and Robert A. Russell for improving my understanding of these matters.)

Divine Affirmations

by Sondra Ray

written after reading
The Door of Everything
with permission of the publisher

1. I am willing to empty out my heart and let God fill it with eternal truth.
2. My yearnings are intense to manifest anything the Father has. The desires of my heart are fulfilled.
3. I am ready to be pulled through the door of everything!
4. I accept eternal perfection and I am mastering the surface mind.
5. I now empty myself out to receive the Spirit. I am now filled with light.
6. I am created in the image and likeness of God.
7. I am a grand Cosmic Being with the ability to come and go with the speed of thought.
8. I am created by the pattern of living Christ.
9. I now elevate the Christ mind and let it express.
10. I take up residence with God.
11. I now experience all wisdom, love and power.
12. I am now master of the elements and master of my body.
13. I stand forth in full expression and my body is as indestructible as Jesus.
14. I can now teleport, dematerialize and rematerialize at will.
15. My body can carry the high potency of my Holy Spirit.
16. I can easily unlearn wrong ideas.
17. I let go of old ideas now.
18. My body is now made new.
19. I am like a bright star!
20. I am given words to shout the glorious truth.
21. I am now willing to trust my future.
22. The truth grows and ripens within me. It is watered with faith and nourished with prayers.
23. I am lifted off the wheel and set free.
24. I go about the business of the Father Consciousness.
25. Nothing else matters except God's will be done.

26. I have no concern for tomorrow.
27. I completely let go of the ego self.
28. I keep the image of myself as the Living Christ.
29. I cast away old habits and doubts.
30. My Christ pattern within is now released.
31. My soul finds expression through this body.
32. My body receives the life force. My heart lets it all in.
33. I am wedded to the light of Christ.
34. I appreciate the spark of life.
35. I allow the light of life to come forward and increase.
36. The surge of life in me safely multiplies by the thousands.
37. My physical body is transmuted into quickened, refined substance.
38. I am now filled with the Holy Spirit.
39. I am born again.
40. I open wide my mind and heart to receive greater amounts of the life force.
41. I catch cosmic rays.
42. My eye is single to the glory of God and my whole body is filled with light.
43. My submerged mind is awake and I can now transmute the Holy Spirit.
44. I am directed by the wisdom of the soul.
45. My surface mind is oriented only towards God's glory.
46. I show my brother what he can do.
47. I hungrily receive the Holy Spirit.
48. I am now washed clean of all negativity.
49. Even my brain cells are replaced with new cells.
50. Since I am pure in heart and pure in mind, I can receive the fulfillment of the Holy Spirit.
51. My strong faith radiates outward.
52. I am exalted to the Christ level of consciousness.
53. My endocrine glands transform me to immortality.
54. I hunger and thirst after the light of Christ.
55. I am now filled with light.
56. My surface mind is now purified by the Holy Spirit.
57. My cells are now repaired. Tired tissue is replaced. My bloodstream is purified.
58. I am a vibration of love.
59. The pineal gland is the spiritual center, and mine is reawakened and very active.
60. I now experience extended vision.

61. God's special rays radiate from me, penetrating all surfaces.
62. The center of power within my throat is fully awakened and my words ring out.
63. I can now perform the miracles of Jesus.
64. My words are backed by God's power.
65. I am master of the atomic elements—master of the flesh.
66. The sick are automatically healed as I pass by.
67. A soft, exquisite radiance surrounds me.
68. I am clothed by the light.
69. I am ready to surrender completely to God's will.
70. Thank you, Father, that I am blended with your Spirit.
71. The manna of the Holy Spirit fills me and I am ready to do the works Jesus said I could do.
72. I freely relinquish the surface (ego) mind.
73. My physiology is perfect in God.
74. I now re-unify with God and live upward.
75. My heart is filled with love, praise and gratitude.
76. I put my hand in God. I pray without ceasing.
77. I have regained the lost art of prayer.
78. I love God with all my heart, mind and soul.
79. Love naturally floods my mind and heart.
80. The light of Christ within me is brighter every day.
81. I give up fear and evil.
82. I forgive all my brothers.
83. I silently hold the vision of Christ in my brother and sister.
84. I keep my mind centered on the greatest good of all.
85. I relax into the awareness of God's presence.
86. I live and breathe the ascension attitudes: love, praise, and gratitude.
87. I focus my thoughts on the exalted Christ level.
88. I fill my head with praise.
89. Gratitude is my natural reaction to life.
90. I give thanks for my senses so I can enjoy God's world.
91. I give thanks for the things I want that I am about to receive.
92. I unlock the Door of Everything.
93. I do not dwell on problems. I contemplate only God and life.
94. I no longer judge by appearances.
95. I awake the Father Consciousness.
96. My thoughts and feelings are focused on everlasting perfection.
97. I sow love and perfection.

98. I ask the Father for the gifts of the Holy Spirit and He gives them to me: Life in Immortality! Brightness in righteousness! Truth in full assurance!
99. I have faith to bring about things beyond reason.
100. My desires become experience with the speed of thought.
101. My faith is set in motion.
102. I use my faith to invite the unfoldment of the sacred pattern in my soul.
103. I live at the Christhood level and miracles happen every day.
104. My heart is opened wide and ready to be filled with light.
105. My one goal is to live upward so God's will can be done.
106. My healing occurs spontaneously.
107. I am now reaching the state of total stillness.
108. I am an authentic teacher of truth and lean completely on His strength.
109. I surrender in humble stillness.
110. I pray for quieting of turbulence.
111. God's voice vibrates in me like music and I hear the message accurately.
112. I am intoxicated with His guidance.
113. My body overcomes the earthy vibrations and is transmuted into light so that I can dematerialize and rematerialize.
114. I can be with loved ones at the speed of thought.
115. I rise above the trap of death!
116. I put God above all things and surrender without the slightest reservation to God's will.
117. My light of Christ is increasing every minute of every day.
118. Christ love changes every imperfection in me to perfection.
119. I am alive now, therefore my life urges are stronger than my death urges. As long as I go on strengthening my life urges and weakening my death urges, I will go on living in perfect health and youthfulness.
120. I allow the Holy Spirit to undo all the wrong thinking that would keep me from having these affirmations manifest.

The God Training
(The Loving Relationships Spiritual Retreat)

INCLUDES:

Teachings of Babaji

Chanting/Prayers/Meditations

Course in Miracles Studies and Application

Advanced Work on Holy Relationships

Spiritual Healing and Rejuvenation

Immortality and Transmutation

Balinese Influences

Wet and Dry Rebirthings

Indian Sweats (depending on location)

World Peace Matters

Other Spiritual Influences

This is a seven day training

For additional information:

1-800-468-5578

or

1-203-354-8509

ABOUT THE LRT

The LRT is the Loving Relationships Training. A weekend work-shop, this magical gathering empowers you to raise your self-esteem, locate and release unconscious negative patterns, and apply the patterns of spiritual enlightenment towards practical life changes. At the LRT you transform your relationships with your-self, your family, your mate, your body, your career and God. It is unique in that it helps you to see how your birth script influences all your major relationships and how the unconscious death urge can sabotage you without your knowing it. For further information contact LRT International, P.O. Box 1465, Washington, CT 06793, (800) INT'L LRT, (203) 354-8509.

OTHER BOOKS BY SONDRA RAY
AVAILABLE FROM CELESTIAL ARTS . . .

The Only Diet There Is—use the power of the mind to transform your attitudes about eating and change your life. 156 pages. $7.95

Celebration of Breath—the basic steps we can take in life to produce well-being and longevity. 204 pages. $8.95

Loving Relationships—how to find and keep the most fulfilling rela-tionships you can imagine, using affirmations. 192 pages. $7.95

Inner Communion—find the deep, spiritual side of your nature. 144 pages. $7.95

Pure Joy—a guide to many spiritual practices that will guide us on our upward paths. 192 pages. $9.95

How to Be Chic, Fabulous, and Live Forever—immortalist philoso-phies are explored in a fascinating guide to longevity. 240 pages, hardbound only. $18.95

Ideal Birth—prevent prenatal birth trauma to newborns by creating the ideal, and consciously aware birth style. 300 pages. $8.95

I Deserve Love—use affirmations to achieve whatever goals you pursue. 128 pages. $7.95